Editorials

ジャパンタイムズ
社説集

2020年

1月▶6月

編▶
ジャパンタイムズ出版 英語出版編集部

上半期

January to June 2020

the japan
times
出版

⫸ 2020年上半期の世界と日本

1月

● **日産のゴーン元会長、国際指名手配**
不法出国し、中東レバノンへ逃亡。日本は国際刑事警察機構(ICPO)を通じて手配を要請。

● **イランによる米軍基地の報復攻撃、米国は経済制裁を表明**
米トランプ大統領がイランへの追加の経済制裁を発表。軍事衝突は当面回避。

● **新型肺炎、国内で初めて確認**
厚生労働省が、中国・湖北省武漢市に渡航した30代男性の新型コロナウイルス陽性反応を発表。

● **千葉の地層・地質時代名に「チバニアン」が正式決定**
約77万年前から13万年前の地質時代を、千葉時代を意味するチバニアンと命名へ。

● **英ヘンリー王子夫妻、主要王族から退く意向**
今後公務には参加せず、財政的な自立を目指すという夫妻の考えをエリザベス女王も容認。

● **三菱電機に大規模サイバー攻撃、機密情報流出の恐れ**
中国系サイバー攻撃集団が関与したと見られ、個人情報や企業機密流出の可能性も。

● **米NBAの元スター選手、コービー・ブライアント氏がヘリコプター墜落事故死**
ロサンゼルス・レイカーズで1996年から20年間活躍、1試合81得点など数々の偉業を達成したスター選手が不慮の死。

● **中国国内での新型コロナ感染者数がSARS超え**
国家衛生健康委員会(NHC)が2002〜03年流行のSARS感染者数を、新型コロナウイルス感染者数が上回った(5,974人)と発表。

● **幕尻の力士・徳勝龍、14勝1敗で初優勝**
大相撲初場所で、幕内で最下位の徳勝龍が優勝。

2月

● **英国、欧州連合(EU)を正式に離脱**
国民の半数が「残留」を支持する中、47年間加盟していたEUからの離脱を正式決定。

● **客船ダイヤモンド・プリンセス号で新型コロナ集団感染**
香港で下船した乗客の感染が確認された後、横浜港で隔離状態となったクルーズ船内で感染者が急増。

● **米トランプ大統領、弾劾裁判で無罪判決へ**
「ウクライナ疑惑」をめぐる弾劾裁判で、上院が無罪判決。

● **韓国映画『パラサイト』がアカデミー賞作品賞など4部門制覇**
韓国の『パラサイト 半地下の家族』がアジア映画初の作品賞。英語圏以外の作品で史上初の快挙。

● **プロ野球の名監督・野村克也氏、84歳で死去**
現役時代は捕手として活躍し、戦後初の三冠王を獲得。南海、ヤクルト、阪神、楽天の監督を歴任した。

● **オーストラリアの森林火災、制圧宣言**
約6カ月続いた大規模森林火災が鎮火。12万平方キロ余りが焼失し、野生動物約10億匹が犠牲に。

● **相模原「津久井やまゆり園」事件、被告に死刑求刑**
2016年に重度障害者19人が殺害された事件の裁判員裁判で、元職員・植松被告に死刑求刑。刑は3月に確定。

● **米とタリバン、和平合意に署名**
2001年からのアフガニスタン戦争をめぐり、米国と旧支配勢力タリバンが和平合意。

● **マレーシア第8代首相にムヒディン氏**
辞任したマハティール首相の側近、元副首相のムヒディン・ヤシン氏が新首相に。

3月

● **大相撲春場所、戦後初の無観客開催**
新型コロナウイルス感染拡大防止および政府見解を受け、決定。

● **穏健派バイデン前副大統領、スーパーチューズデーで10州制す**
米大統領選の民主党候補指名争いで、テキサス州などで勝利。獲得代議員数トップに。

● **WHO、新型コロナのパンデミックを宣言**
114の国・地域で、感染者約11万8,000人超、死者4,291人に上ったことを受け、世界的な流行に危機感を表明。

● **山手線、高輪ゲートウェイ駅開業**
品川—田町間に山手線では49年ぶりとなる新駅が開設。

● **東京オリンピック・パラリンピックの延期が決定**
国際オリンピック委員会(IOC)は7月24日開幕予定であった同大会の開催を「1年程度」遅らせると発表。

● **英ジョンソン首相がコロナに感染**
ウイルス陽性が判明後、官邸内で自主隔離しつつビデオ会議などで公務を遂行。

● **伊、新型コロナの死者が1万人を突破**
2月に流行し始めて以来、感染者が急増したイタリアで、死者が世界で初めて1万人を超えた。

4月

● **テニスのウィンブルドン選手権が中止に**
新型コロナウイルスの感染拡大を受け、中止が決定。サッカーの欧州選手権なども予定変更。

● **安倍首相、全世帯に布マスク2枚配布へ**
日本郵便のシステムを使い、新型コロナウイルス感染拡大地域から順次配布開始すると表明。

● **英エリザベス女王、国民へビデオメッセージ**
特別演説にて、新型コロナウイルスの危機は必ず克服できると呼び掛け。

● **緊急事態宣言発令**
感染症拡大を踏まえ、政府は東京、大阪など7都府県で緊急事態措置を取ると発表。

● **Zoom、セキュリティーの脆弱性が明らかに**
利用者急増のオンライン会議システムで、Zoombombing(ズーム爆撃)と呼ばれる悪質行為が多発。

● **武漢、2カ月半ぶりに都市封鎖(ロックダウン)解除**
中国・武漢市で高速鉄道や高速道路などの運用、航空会社の運航が再開。

● **安倍首相、一人当たり10万円の一律給付を正式表明**
減収世帯への30万円支給案を取り下げ、全国民への給付に切り替えることを決定。

5月

厚労省、レムデシビルを承認
米製薬会社の抗ウイルス薬が、新型コロナウイルス治療薬として国内で初承認。

検察庁法改正案、今国会での成立を断念
検察幹部の定年を最長3年延長できる特例に世論が強く反発。政府・与党は採決を見送り。

夏の甲子園大会、中止決定
全国高校野球選手権が戦後初の開催中止。

ウクライナのゼレンスキー大統領、就任1年
就任1年で、ウクライナ東部紛争の終結と汚職撲滅の重要公約を果たす。

黒川検事長、賭けマージャンを認め、辞表を提出
緊急事態宣言下に新聞記者らと賭けマージャンを行っていたことによる引責辞任。

テニスの大坂なおみ選手、世界で最も稼いだ女性アスリートに
米経済誌『フォーブス』が、同選手の年間総収入額が女子アスリート史上最高の約40億円と報道。

女子プロレスラーの木村花さん、急死
恋愛リアリティー番組『テラスハウス』出演者の突然の死に、ネット上での誹謗中傷が社会問題化。

米国で警官の拘束下、黒人男性が死亡
米ミネアポリスでジョージ・フロイド氏が逮捕時に警官に首を圧迫されて死亡。黒人差別に抗議するデモが拡大。

京アニ放火殺人事件、容疑者逮捕
36人が亡くなった京都アニメーション放火事件の容疑者が入院先の病室で逮捕。

6月

● **「東京アラート」発動**
　新型コロナウイルス感染拡大の兆しが見られるとして、東京都が警戒を促す。

● **藤井聡太七段、史上最年少でタイトル挑戦権獲得**
　棋聖戦の挑戦者を決定するトーナメントを勝ち抜き、最年少記録を31年ぶりに更新。

● **40年以上にわたり拉致問題解決を訴えた横田滋さん、死去**
　北朝鮮に拉致された横田めぐみさんの父、滋さんが老衰のため87歳で死去。

● **世界経済、第二次世界大戦以来最悪の景気後退に**
　新型コロナウイルス感染症を封じ込めるための経済活動停止措置により、2020年の世界経済成長率はマイナス5.2%になるとの予測。

● **サンリオ、創業初の社長交代**
　創業者の孫である辻朋邦専務(31歳)の昇格が決定。

● **北朝鮮、南北共同連絡事務所を爆破**
　韓国の脱北者団体が金正恩朝鮮労働党委員長を批判するビラを散布したことに対する報復措置。

● **米連邦最高裁、LGBTQに対する雇用差別を違法と判断**
　最高裁判事9人中6人が公民権法の性的マイノリティーへの適用を支持。

● **河井克行前法相夫妻、買収容疑で逮捕**
　2019年7月の参院選で、広島の地元議員らに計約2570万円を配ったとして、公職選挙法違反容疑。

● **プロ野球、新型コロナで3カ月遅れのシーズン開幕**
　セ・パ両リーグ、開幕戦は史上初の無観客試合に。

● 監修・執筆者紹介

又江原 裕　またえばら・ゆたか

1935年生まれ。早稲田大学政治経済学部卒業。
ジャパンタイムズ論説顧問。
同社編集局長、主幹、専務などを歴任後、現職。

● 翻訳・語注執筆者紹介（50音順）

宇都宮 まどか　うつのみや・まどか

1968年生まれ。州立カリフォルニア大学バークレー校政治学科卒業。ジャパンタイムズ
「週刊ST」、「Japan Times Weekly」主任を経て、翻訳者、英語学習アドバイザー。
訳書に『英語で読むからよくわかる チューデイ先生のなるほど英語レッスン超基本編』
（ジャパンタイムズ出版）。

桑田 健　くわた・たけし

1965年生まれ。東京外国語大学英米語学科卒業。
訳書に『痛いほど君が好きなのに』（ヴィレッジブックス）、『マギの聖骨』『AIの魔女』などの
「シグマフォース・シリーズ」、「THE HUNTERSシリーズ」、「タッカー＆ケイン・シリーズ」
（以上、竹書房）、『地球 驚異の自然現象』（河出書房）、『ビッグデータベースボール』『ア
ストロボール』『プロジェクト・ネメシス』『プロジェクト・マイゴ』（以上、KADOKAWA）、
『セックス・イン・ザ・シー』（講談社）などがある。

小川 貴宏　こかわ・たかひろ

1962年生まれ。東京外国語大学英米語学科卒業。
同大学修士課程（ゲルマン系言語専攻）修了。英国Exeter Universityで応用言語学修士
号を取得。防衛大学校准教授を経て、現在、成蹊大学教授。
著書に『Sound Right! 14のグループで覚える英語の発音』、翻訳・解説執筆に『英語で見
る！ 聴く！ BBCドキュメンタリー＆ドラマ BOOK 1』（以上、ジャパンタイムズ出版）がある。

中村 直子　なかむら・なおこ

1951年生まれ。上智大学英米文学科卒業。
元ジャパンタイムズ「週刊ST」副編集長。
翻訳・解説執筆に『英語で読む旧約聖書』『英語で読む新約聖書』、編著書に『身の回りのこ
とが何でも言える 英会話ぷち表現』、訳書に『英語で読む源氏物語（上）（下）』『英語で読
む平家物語（上）（下）』『英語で読む古典落語』『英語で読む世界昔話 Book 1 〜5』（以上、
ジャパンタイムズ出版）などがある。

2020年上半期の世界と日本 iii

■ 新型コロナウイルスが与えた影響

① **COVID-19: Preventing a medical system breakdown**
.... 02　**Tracks 02-05**

新型コロナウイルス感染症による医療崩壊を防ぐ　>> 2020年2月27日

② **The challenges we face for the 2021 Tokyo Games**
.... 10　**Tracks 06-09**

2021年東京五輪開催に向けた課題　>> 2020年3月26日

③ **A crucial time to keep coronavirus crisis under control** .... 18　**Tracks 10-14**

今がコロナウイルス危機を抑え込めるかどうかの正念場　>> 2020年4月9日

④ **Government's support for schools is essential**
.... 26　**Tracks 15-19**

新型コロナ休校中、国の支援が不可欠　>> 2020年4月16日

⑤ **Extend support for foreign students in Japan**
.... 34　**Tracks 20-25**

日本にいる外国人留学生に支援の手を　>> 2020年4月30日

⑥ **Shore up Japan's weakened health care system**
.... 42　**Tracks 26-30**

日本の弱体化した医療制度を強化する　>> 2020年5月7日

⑦ **The state of emergency is lifted: What's next?**
.... 50　**Tracks 31-36**

緊急事態宣言解除、次に取るべき方策とは　>> 2020年5月29日

訳 58

特別掲載 **Will 'flu' come back?** .... 72　**Tracks 37-40**

>> 1919年10月23日【100年前の社説】

■■ その他の社会問題

① **Broaden the fight against demographic woes**
.... 80　**Tracks 41-45**

人口統計学的な難局との闘いを広げよ　>> 2020年1月9日

② **Coming to terms with what's behind the Sagamihara killings**.. 90　**Tracks 46-49**

相模原障害者施設殺傷事件の背後にある問題　>> 2020年2月13日

③ **Review the nation's quest for a nuclear fuel cycle**
.... 96　**Tracks 50-53**

見直すべき核燃料サイクルの探求　>> 2020年2月20日

④ **Online abuse is a silent pandemic affecting millions**
.... 102　**Tracks 54-60**

ネット上の中傷は多くを苦しめる静かなパンデミック　>> 2020年6月11日

訳 110

エディター／霜村 和久
編集協力／堀内 友子
カバーデザイン／日下 充典
本文デザイン／ハーモナイズデザイン（松森 雅孝、柳沢 由美子）
写真提供／共同通信社
ナレーター／クリス・コプロウスキー、ハンナ・グレース

●音声収録時間／約62分

音声のご利用案内

本書に掲載されているすべての英文記事の読み上げ音声を、無料でダウンロードし、お聞きいただくことができます。

スマートフォン

1. ジャパンタイムズ出版の音声アプリ「OTO Navi」をインストール

2. OTO Naviで本書を検索
3. 音声をダウンロードし、再生

3秒早送り・早戻し、繰り返し再生などの便利機能つき。
学習にお役立てください。

パソコン

1. ブラウザからジャパンタイムズ出版のサイト「BOOK CLUB」にアクセス
   https://bookclub.japantimes.co.jp/book/b524495.html
2. 「ダウンロード」ボタンをクリック
3. 音声をダウンロードし、iTunesなどに取り込んで再生

※音声はzipファイルを展開(解凍)してご利用ください。

新型コロナウイルスが
与えた影響

3月27日、東京オリンピック1年延期決定後、記者会見するIOCバッハ会長

COVID-19: Preventing a medical system breakdown

新型コロナウイルス感染症による医療崩壊を防ぐ

February 27, 2020　　　　　　　　●Tracks 02-05 / 訳 pp. 58-59

`Track 02`

1　　Japan finds itself at a critical juncture for the next week or two in the effort to prevent a rapid increase in domestic infections of the COVID-19 coronavirus, according to a panel of infectious disease experts who are advising the government. Yet the government's basic policies released earlier this week—which essentially follow guidelines already announced by the health ministry—do not appear to share that sense of crisis. Efforts to contain the domestic outbreak of COVID-19 can attain greater speed by anticipating and taking steps to avoid a worst-case scenario in which the nation's medical system collapses under the weight of mass infections.

2　　The focus of the fight against COVID-19 has shifted from a prevention of cross-border infections to forestalling a mass domestic outbreak. A panel of experts has stated that the priority now is to curb an increase in new infections and minimize the number of people who develop serious symptoms that can lead to fatalities. The panel has warned of the possibility of mass infections being unknowingly spread by infected individuals, and urges everyone to refrain from attending gatherings and events where they will be in close contact with large numbers of people over an extended period.

日本は、新型コロナウイルスの感染急増を防ぐ上で重大な岐路にさしかかっている。政府は、国の医療崩壊という最悪のシナリオを想定し、それを回避する措置を講じて、感染症を封じ込める取り組みを迅速化すべきだ。

1
- □ [タイトル]COVID-19 →新型コロナウイルス感染症の正式名称。COはCorona、VIはVirus、DはDiseaseから。19は発生が確認された2019年が由来
- □ [タイトル]prevent 防ぐ
- □ [タイトル]medical system 医療制度
- □ [タイトル]breakdown 崩壊
- □ critical 重大な
- □ juncture 岐路
- □ domestic 国内の
- □ infection 感染
- □ panel 委員会
- □ infectious disease 感染症
- □ advise 勧告する
- □ basic policy 基本方針
- □ essentially 基本的に
- □ share 共有する
- □ sense of crisis 危機感
- □ contain 封じ込める、阻止する
- □ outbreak 発生、大流行
- □ attain 達成する
- □ anticipate 予測する
- □ avoid 回避する
- □ worst-case scenario 最悪のシナリオ
- □ under the weight of ... …の重圧で
- □ mass 大規模な

2
- □ focus 焦点
- □ shift 移る
- □ cross-border 国境を越える
- □ forestall 未然に防ぐ
- □ state 述べる
- □ priority 優先事項
- □ curb 抑制する
- □ minimize 最小限に抑える
- □ serious symptom 重篤な症状
- □ fatality 死亡
- □ warn 警告する
- □ unknowingly 気付かずに
- □ individual 個人
- □ urge 要請する
- □ refrain from *doing* ～することを控える
- □ attend 出席する
- □ gathering 集会
- □ close contact 濃厚接触
- □ over an extended period 長時間にわたって

Track 03

3 In the basic policies unveiled Tuesday, however, the government said it would not uniformly call on organizers to cancel or postpone such events, but instead ask them to think twice about the necessity of the gatherings—wording that reportedly reflected the government's aversion to discouraging economic activities. But on Wednesday, Prime Minister Shinzo Abe said that the government is now requesting that sports and cultural events involving large numbers of participants over the coming two weeks be canceled, delayed or scaled down.

4 Given the spike in infections among people who have no recent history of travel to China—where the outbreak originated—a major challenge going forward will be to prevent the collapse of medical services for treating COVID-19 patients and others.

Track 04

5 So far, people infected with the new coronavirus are being cared for at hospitals designated for treating infectious diseases that are equipped with airtight facilities to prevent an outflow of viruses. But many of these medical institutions in the greater Tokyo area are now filled with hundreds of patients who were infected aboard the cruise ship Diamond Princess, raising concerns over a shortage of artificial respirators needed for treating COVID-19 patients who have developed pneumonia. A warning has been issued stating that an escalation in mass infections under such circumstances would overwhelm the capacity of these medical institutions, placing at risk patients—including those suffering from other illnesses—whose lives could be saved in normal circumstances.

3
- ☐ unveil 発表する
- ☐ uniformly 一律に
- ☐ call on ... to *do* …に〜するように訴える、求める
- ☐ organizer 主催者
- ☐ cancel 中止する
- ☐ postpone 延期する
- ☐ think twice よく考える
- ☐ necessity 必要性
- ☐ wording 表現

- ☐ reportedly 報じられるところによれば
- ☐ reflect 反映する
- ☐ aversion 嫌悪感、抵抗感
- ☐ discourage 妨げる
- ☐ economic activity 経済活動
- ☐ participant 参加者
- ☐ coming 来るべき
- ☐ delay 延期する
- ☐ scale down 規模を縮小する

4
- ☐ given …を考えると
- ☐ spike 急激な上昇
- ☐ history of travel 渡航歴
- ☐ originate 始まる、起こる

- ☐ major 主要な
- ☐ challenge 課題
- ☐ going forward 今後の
- ☐ treat 治療する

5
- ☐ so far 今までのところ
- ☐ new coronavirus 新型コロナウイルス
- ☐ care for ... …の手当てをする
- ☐ designate for ... …に指定する
- ☐ be equipped with ... …を備える
- ☐ airtight facility 気密施設
- ☐ outflow 流出
- ☐ the greater Tokyo area 首都圏
- ☐ be filled with ... …でいっぱいになる
- ☐ aboard …に乗って
- ☐ cruise ship クルーズ船
- ☐ raise concerns 不安を引き起こす
- ☐ shortage 不足
- ☐ artificial respirator 人工呼吸器

- ☐ develop 発症する
- ☐ pneumonia 肺炎
- ☐ escalation 拡大
- ☐ circumstance(s) 状況
- ☐ overwhelm 圧倒する
- ☐ capacity 収容能力
- ☐ place at risk 危険にさらす
- ☐ patient 患者
- ☐ including …を含む
- ☐ suffer from ... …を患っている
- ☐ illness 病気
- ☐ save 救う
- ☐ normal 通常の

6   Under the government's basic policies, in areas that have witnessed a sharp increase in the number of COVID-19 patients, hospitals that are not designated for treating infectious disease patients will be asked to accept people with possible coronavirus infections on the condition that they be kept isolated from other patients. Reports show that undesignated hospitals in many parts of the country are not prepared to accept COVID-19 patients under these conditions. Efforts must be expedited to establish guidelines for these hospitals so they can take the necessary steps to accept such patients safely and avert a concentration of many possibly infected people at a small number of hospitals.

Track 05

7   Everyone has a role to play in preventing the spread of COVID-19. People who fear they might be infected but do not have serious symptoms should refrain from going to medical institutions, which would use valuable medical resources that are needed by people who are actually ill and also raise the risk of further spreading the disease. Experts on infectious diseases warn that medical institutions can become incubators for mass infections. The government must introduce concrete measures to ensure that, as its basic policies call for, people with mild, cold-like symptoms can feel secure staying at home instead of visiting hospitals.

6
- □ area 地域
- □ witness 経験する
- □ sharp 急激な
- □ accept 受け入れる
- □ on the condition that ... …という条件で
- □ isolate 隔離する
- □ report 報告、報道
- □ show 示す
- □ undesignated 非指定の
- □ be prepared to *do* ～する準備ができた
- □ expedite 早める
- □ establish 確立する
- □ necessary 必要な
- □ avert 回避する
- □ concentration 集中
- □ possibly ひょっとしたら

7
- □ role to play 果たすべき役割
- □ spread 拡大
- □ fear 恐れる
- □ valuable 貴重な
- □ medical resource(s) 医療資源
- □ actually 実際に
- □ ill 病気の
- □ raise 高める
- □ further さらに
- □ incubator 培養器
- □ introduce 導入する
- □ concrete measure(s) 具体的措置
- □ ensure 確実にする
- □ call for ... …を掲げる
- □ mild 軽い
- □ cold-like 風邪のような
- □ secure 安全な
- □ stay at home 家にとどまる
- □ instead of ... …の代わりに

8　One way to ease people's sense of insecurity over the outbreak would be to increase the availability of COVID-19 virus tests— the supply of which is limited. That would allow more people to take tests and stop them from unknowingly spreading the disease. Health minister Katsunobu Kato told the Diet on Wednesday that an average of roughly 900 tests for the new virus were performed daily over the previous week—far below the daily maximum of 3,800 tests that the government earlier said would be possible. The relevant authorities should resolve the problems that have hampered an increase in the supply of virus tests and take steps— including the greater use of private sector resources—to make them available for all people who wish to take them.

8
- □ one way 一つの方法
- □ ease 和らげる
- □ sense of insecurity 不安感
- □ availability 利用できること
- □ supply 供給
- □ limited 限られた
- □ allow... to *do* …に〜することを許可する
- □ health minister 厚生労働大臣
- □ the Diet 国会
- □ average 平均
- □ roughly おおよそ
- □ perform 行う
- □ daily 毎日
- □ previous week 前の週
- □ far below はるかに下回る
- □ maximum 上限、最大値
- □ relevant 関係する
- □ authorities 当局
- □ resolve 解決する
- □ hamper 妨げる
- □ private sector 民間部門

The challenges we face for the 2021 Tokyo Games

2021年東京五輪開催に向けた課題

March 26, 2020　　　　　　　●Tracks 06-09 / 訳 pp. 60-61

Track 06

1　Postponing the Tokyo Olympic and Paralympic Games for up to a year until summer 2021 was unavoidable given the growth of the coronavirus pandemic gripping the world, but it is a rational decision that will hopefully ensure fairness for all athletes taking part. Now efforts should shift to organizing the games next year in an environment that is safe for not just the athletes but all of the officials and spectators expected from around the globe.

2　Even as the International Olympic Committee said just last week that the games would go ahead as planned, it was becoming increasingly clear this would be impossible. The number of people infected with COVID-19 worldwide topped 400,000 this week— double the number of just a week earlier—and more than 20,000 people have died. There was no prospect that the pandemic would subside by July so that Japan, even if it manages to get its domestic outbreak under control, could welcome a huge crowd of spectators to the games. Following the decision, the World Health Organization said it had warned Japan and the IOC that going ahead with the 2020 Games would have exacerbated the pandemic even further.

国際オリンピック委員会は3月24日、7月から開催予定だった東京オリンピック・パラリンピックを1年程度延期すると発表した。新型コロナウイルス感染拡大を受けた措置で、五輪史上初の延期となる。変更に伴う課題は多岐にわたり、日本経済への打撃も懸念される。

1
- ☐ [タイトル]challenge 課題
- ☐ [タイトル]face 直面する
- ☐ postpone 延期する
- ☐ up to ... 最長で…
- ☐ unavoidable 避けられない、やむを得ない
- ☐ given …を考慮すると
- ☐ coronavirus コロナウイルス（の）
- ☐ pandemic （疫病の）世界的大流行
- ☐ grip 席巻する
- ☐ rational 合理的な
- ☐ ensure 確保する
- ☐ fairness 公平性
- ☐ take part 参加する
- ☐ effort 取り組み
- ☐ official 当局者
- ☐ spectator 観客
- ☐ around the globe 世界中

2
- ☐ even as ... …にもかかわらず
- ☐ International Olympic Committee 国際オリンピック委員会
- ☐ go ahead 進む
- ☐ as planned 予定通り
- ☐ increasingly ますます
- ☐ impossible 不可能な
- ☐ infected with ... …に感染した
- ☐ COVID-19 新型コロナウイルス感染症 →Corona Virus Disease 2019の略
- ☐ worldwide 世界中で
- ☐ top 超える
- ☐ double 2倍の
- ☐ just a week earlier そのわずか1週間前
- ☐ more than ... …を超える
- ☐ prospect 見込み、めど
- ☐ subside 収束する
- ☐ manage to *do* 何とかして〜する
- ☐ get ... under control …を抑制する
- ☐ domestic 国内の
- ☐ outbreak 大流行
- ☐ welcome 迎え入れる
- ☐ huge crowd of ... 大勢の…
- ☐ following …を受けて
- ☐ World Health Organization 世界保健機関
- ☐ warn 警告する
- ☐ exacerbate 深刻化させる
- ☐ even further さらにもっと

3　Pressure from athletes and sports organizations worldwide was building on the IOC to postpone the games, with the national Olympic committees of some countries saying they would not send their athletes to Tokyo if the games were to start in July as scheduled. The pandemic has deprived the athletes of a chance to prepare for the games in optimum conditions. Other major international sports events have been called off, and the cancellation of qualifying events have left the selection of more than 40 percent of the roughly 11,000 athletes who are expected to compete in the Tokyo Olympics undetermined. Holding the games this summer would have been unfair as it would have deprived many athletes of a level playing field.

4　Still, the unprecedented task of rescheduling the Olympic Games—which have been canceled five times in their 124-year history, each time due to war, including the 1940 games that were to be held in Tokyo—will involve massive challenges. First among them will be making sure that the COVID-19 pandemic is contained by the time the games are held next year—a task whose accomplishment is far from guaranteed. The safety of the athletes, sports officials, spectators and everybody else involved from around the world will continue to be the priority in organizing the games.

3
- ☐ sports organization 競技団体
- ☐ build 高まる
- ☐ national Olympic committee 国内オリンピック委員会
- ☐ send 派遣する
- ☐ if ... were to *do* …が仮に〜するとしたら
- ☐ as scheduled 予定通りに
- ☐ deprive A of B AからBを奪う
- ☐ prepare for ... …の準備をする
- ☐ optimum condition 最高の状態
- ☐ major 大規模な
- ☐ call off 取りやめる
- ☐ cancellation 中止
- ☐ qualifying event 予選大会→ここでは、オリンピック・パラリンピック出場資格を得るための大会
- ☐ leave ... undetermined 未定のままにする
- ☐ selection 選考
- ☐ roughly およそ
- ☐ be expected to *do* 〜することが見込まれる
- ☐ compete 競う
- ☐ hold 開催する
- ☐ unfair 不公平な
- ☐ level playing field 公平な競争の場

4
- ☐ still とはいえ、それでも
- ☐ unprecedented 前例のない
- ☐ reschedule スケジュールを組み直す
- ☐ each time 各回
- ☐ due to ... …が原因で
- ☐ including …を含めて
- ☐ 1940 games 1940年東京オリンピック→日中戦争の影響などから中止となった
- ☐ involve 伴う
- ☐ massive 大量の
- ☐ first among them その最初の一つ
- ☐ contain 抑え込む
- ☐ by the time ... …までに
- ☐ accomplishment 達成
- ☐ far from ... …には程遠い
- ☐ guaranteed 保証された
- ☐ safety 安全
- ☐ everybody else その他の人々
- ☐ ... involved 関係している…
- ☐ priority 優先事項

Track 08

5   The challenges will range from coordinating the schedules for other international sports contests set to be held next year, securing the venues for each of the events in the 2021 Olympics, rearranging accommodations and transportation for participants and reorganizing tens of thousands of volunteer staff who will help run the games.

6   Ensuring fairness in selecting the athletes to compete in the games—if the process needs to be redone due to the delay—will also be important. Postponing the Olympics is expected to entail massive additional expenses to the tune of hundreds of billions of yen. Who will pay for this—and how—needs to be quickly determined.

Track 09

7   The delay will push back the economic benefits associated with the Olympics. This will add to the woes of the Japanese economy, which is already being battered by the effects of the pandemic, including a nosedive in inbound tourism, and is widely feared to be headed into a prolonged recession. The government must take steps to contain the economic damage while combating the spread of domestic COVID-19 infections, including in Tokyo, which just as the postponement was announced was described as "at significant risk of further outbreaks."

5
- [ ] range from A, B, C, and D A、B、C、そして、Dにまで及ぶ
- [ ] coordinate 調整する
- [ ] contest 競技会
- [ ] set to *do* 〜することになっている
- [ ] secure 確保する
- [ ] venue 会場
- [ ] rearrange 再調整する
- [ ] accommodation 宿泊場所
- [ ] transportation 移動手段
- [ ] participant 参加者
- [ ] reorganize 再編成する
- [ ] tens of thousands of ... 何万もの…
- [ ] run 運営する

6
- [ ] redo やり直す
- [ ] delay 延期
- [ ] entail 必然的に伴う
- [ ] additional 追加の
- [ ] expense 支出
- [ ] to the tune of ... …もの多大な金額
- [ ] hundreds of billions of ... 数千億もの…
- [ ] determine 決定する

7
- [ ] push back 先送りする
- [ ] economic benefits 経済的利益
- [ ] associated with ... …と関連する
- [ ] add to ... …を増大させる
- [ ] woe 悩みの種
- [ ] batter 打ちのめす
- [ ] effect 影響
- [ ] nosedive 激減
- [ ] inbound tourism 訪日観光
- [ ] widely 広く
- [ ] feared 懸念される
- [ ] head into ... …に向かう
- [ ] prolonged 長引く
- [ ] recession 不況
- [ ] take steps 対策を講じる
- [ ] combat 闘う
- [ ] just as ... …と同時に
- [ ] postponement 延期
- [ ] be described as ... …と言い表される
- [ ] at risk 危険にさらされて
- [ ] significant 重大な

8　Prime Minister Shinzo Abe, who has sought to hold the 2020 Games as a key legacy of his long-running administration, is believed to have taken the initiative for postponing them by a year. The IOC's formal decision to put off the Olympics was preceded by an agreement to that effect between Mr. Abe and IOC President Thomas Bach—only two days after the IOC announced that it would reach a conclusion within four weeks. Delaying the games is certainly a better option than the worst-case scenario of having to cancel them. Whether the decision will lead to successfully holding the Olympics next year depends greatly on what Japan can accomplish in the coming months.

8

□ seek to *do* 〜しようと努める

□ key 主な

□ legacy 遺産

□ long-running 長期にわたる

□ administration 政権

□ be believed to *do* 〜すると見られている

□ take initiative 主導する

□ formal 正式な

□ put off 延期する

□ be preceded by ... …が先行する

□ agreement 合意

□ to that effect その趣旨での

□ reach a conclusion 結論を出す

□ within …以内に

□ certainly 確かに

□ better option よりよい選択

□ worst-case scenario 最悪の事態

□ successfully 成功裏に

□ depend greatly on ... …によって大きく左右される

□ accomplish 成し遂げる

□ coming months 今後数カ月

A crucial time to keep coronavirus crisis under control

今がコロナウイルス危機を抑え込めるかどうかの正念場

April 9, 2020　　　　　　　　●Tracks 10-14 / 訳 pp. 62-63

Track 10

1　The state of emergency declared by the government this week due to the rapidly expanding number of coronavirus infections in Tokyo and six other prefectures should cause us not to panic but take the situation seriously. Whether we can get the COVID-19 outbreak under control is up to the behavior of each and every one of us. The government, for its part, needs to ensure there is a safety net to protect the livelihood of people who suffer a lost job or income as the nation combats the pandemic.

2　Unlike the lockdowns being enforced in many major cities in countries experiencing much greater outbreaks, Japan's state of emergency, which lasts through May 6, lacks penalties for not complying with government requests for people in the designated areas to stay at home except for essential or urgent tasks. Whether this step will effectively curb the growing outbreak depends a great deal on how each individual responds.

▼ **About This Editorial** ▼

2019年に発生したとされるコロナウイルスの変種COVID-19は、決定的な治療薬やワクチンもないまま2020年に入って瞬く間に世界中にまん延し、WHOも3月にようやくパンデミック宣言を行った。世界全体が根本的な行動様式の変化を余儀なくされ、経済・社会活動・文化など市民生活に及ぼす影響は計り知れない。

1
- □ [タイトル]keep ... under control …を収束させる、…をうまく抑え込む
- □ [タイトル]coronavirus コロナウイルス→ここでは新型コロナ感染症のこと
- □ state of emergency 緊急事態、非常事態
- □ infection 感染
- □ COVID-19 新型コロナウイルス感染症
- □ outbreak 大流行
- □ up to ... …次第で
- □ behavior 行動
- □ each and every → every の強調表現
- □ for *one's* part ～の側としては
- □ ensure 確実にする
- □ safety net 救済措置
- □ livelihood 生計手段、生活
- □ suffer （被害を）被る
- □ combat …と闘う
- □ pandemic （疫病の）世界的大流行

2
- □ lockdown 都市[地域]封鎖
- □ enforce （強制）執行する
- □ experience 体験する
- □ last through ... …まで続く
- □ comply with ... …に従う
- □ request 要請
- □ designated 指定された
- □ essential 不可欠の
- □ urgent 緊急の
- □ task 仕事、作業
- □ step 方策、措置
- □ effectively 実質的に
- □ curb 抑える
- □ depend a great deal on ... …に大きくかかっている

Track 11

3 Citing experts, the government is asking people to cut back on interactions with others by at least 70 to 80 percent—a move that will hopefully lead to a peak in the infection rate followed by a decline within weeks. How quickly this can be achieved depends on our behavior.

4 The Abe administration is reported to have hesitated for weeks to declare a state of emergency to avoid a further negative impact on the economy, which was already headed for a recession under the weight of the global pandemic. The step will no doubt hit the economy hard as people and businesses curb their activities.

Track 12

5 Along with declaring a state of emergency, the Abe administration adopted a ¥108 trillion economic package to ease the economic pain from the pandemic. It is touted as the largest-ever—indeed it is nearly twice the size of the ¥56 trillion stimulus introduced amid the global financial crisis following the 2008 collapse of Lehman Brothers. But the sheer size of the package—even larger than the government's fiscal 2020 annual budget—aside, its substance must be scrutinized to make sure that sufficient support will be provided to the people most heavily affected—those who lose their job or income in the pandemic.

3
- □ cite …の言葉を引用する
- □ cut back on ... …を減らす
- □ interaction 交流、接触
- □ by →増減の差を表す
- □ move 行動、動き
- □ decline 減少
- □ achieve 達成する

4
- □ administration 政権
- □ be reported to have *done* 報道によると〜したとされて[言われて]いる
- □ hesitate ためらう
- □ further さらなる
- □ negative impact 悪影響
- □ be headed for ... …のほうに向かう
- □ recession 景気後退
- □ weight 重圧
- □ no doubt おそらく、きっと
- □ business 企業

5
- □ along with ... …に加えて
- □ adopt 採択する
- □ trillion 1兆
- □ package 総合[複合]的政策
- □ ease 和らげる
- □ tout 喧伝する
- □ ... -ever これまでで…の
- □ twice the size of ... …の2倍の規模の
- □ stimulus （景気）刺激策
- □ introduce 導入[実行]する
- □ amid …のさなかに
- □ collapse 崩壊
- □ Lehman Brothers →かつての米国の大手投資銀行。2008年、その破綻を発端に世界金融危機が起きた
- □ sheer とてつもない
- □ fiscal …会計年度
- □ annual budget 年度予算
- □ ... aside …はさておき
- □ substance 実質、中身
- □ scrutinize 精査[吟味]する
- □ sufficient 十分な
- □ those who ... …する人々

6   A credible safety net to protect people's livelihood will be a must to ensure the public's cooperation in the fight against the virus, especially as it remains uncertain how long it will last. The economic package must be reviewed and updated to see if it's helping those who really need the support.

`Track 13`

7   The main priority is halting a breakdown in the medical service system, which has already been strained to the brink by the pandemic. The confirmed infections and death toll in Japan may be much smaller than in countries like the United States, Italy, France or Spain, where hundreds of thousands have been infected and more than 10,000 have died. But the fast-accelerating pace of infections in recent days, in particular a sharp increase in the number of patients with untraceable infection routes, has sounded alarms over the possibility of an explosive surge in infections that could cause medical services to collapse.

8   A situation in which the overstretched medical system becomes unable to provide timely treatment for people with severe symptoms must be averted. This week Tokyo officials began moving COVID-19 patients with mild or no symptoms to hotels so medical institutions can focus their limited resources on those with more serious conditions. What must be avoided at all costs, however, is an explosive increase in infections, which could leave not only COVID-19 patients but people with other serious illnesses unable to get the medical help they need.

6
- [ ] credible 信頼できる
- [ ] must 必須事項
- [ ] the public 一般の人々、国民
- [ ] remain …のままである
- [ ] review 見直す
- [ ] see if ... …かどうかを調べる

7
- [ ] halt 止める
- [ ] breakdown 崩壊
- [ ] strain 負担をかける
- [ ] brink 瀬戸際
- [ ] confirm 確認する
- [ ] death toll 死亡者数
- [ ] hundreds of thousands 何十万人
  (もの人々)→このあとに of people が
  省略されている
- [ ] be infected 感染する
- [ ] fast-accelerating 急激に加速していく
- [ ] in particular とりわけ
- [ ] untraceable 経路不明の
- [ ] sound an alarm 警鐘を鳴らす
- [ ] over …に関して
- [ ] explosive 爆発的な
- [ ] surge 急増

8
- [ ] overstretched 過度な負荷のかかった
- [ ] treatment 治療
- [ ] severe (病気が)深刻な
- [ ] symptom 症状
- [ ] avert 避ける、回避する
- [ ] official 当局者
- [ ] mild 軽度の
- [ ] medical institution 医療機関
- [ ] focus A on B A を B に集中させる
- [ ] condition 状態、症状
- [ ] at all costs 何としてでも
- [ ] leave A B A を B の状態のままにする
- [ ] unable to *do* 〜できない

Track 14

9   Whether the nation can succeed in getting the infections under control and avoid such a catastrophe—while containing the damage to the economy and people's livelihood—depends heavily on our own immediate efforts. The government must provide enough support to back these efforts. This will be essential to win the public's trust in the government's response to what may turn out to be a long crisis.

9

- ☐ catastrophe 大惨事
- ☐ contain 抑える
- ☐ immediate 今すぐの
- ☐ back 支える

- ☐ trust in ... …への信頼
- ☐ response to ... …への対応
- ☐ turn out to be ... 結果的に…となる

Government's support for schools is essential

新型コロナ休校中、国の支援が不可欠

April 16, 2020 　　　　　　　　　　●Tracks 15-19 / 訳 pp. 64-65

Track 15

1　More than a week has passed since a state of emergency was declared on April 7 due to the COVID-19 outbreak. However, not everyone seems to be staying home. Data announced by the government showed that the number of people around main stations in the seven designated hot-spot prefectures dropped 40 to 60 percent on Monday compared to average figures in the month from mid-January. This means some people are still commuting to work because of a lack of a telework environment at home or a failure on the part of their companies to change their traditional way of operating, such as a heavy reliance on paper documents and the use of traditional stamps, known as *hanko*, for their approval. This is creating a major divide among companies between those that can sustain their business online and those that cannot.

2　The nation's schools are also increasingly being pressured to go digital as soon as possible. Since most schools in the seven designated prefectures are closed until May 6, the gap between private and public schools has become more evident. While many private schools started to offer online learning programs this month, public schools lag far behind. Moreover, if schools in other areas remain open, a divide will develop between them and those that are closed. The government should provide financial as well as technical support to schools nationwide to help them go digital.

新型コロナウイルス感染拡大防止で休校が長引く中、学習のデジタル化により地域間・学校間での教育格差が広がっている。すべての子どもに平等な教育の機会を与えるために、政府は率先して教育の転換を図り、学校への技術支援や資金援助を行うべきだ。

1
- ☐ [タイトル]essential 必須の
- ☐ state of emergency 緊急事態
- ☐ declare 宣言する
- ☐ due to ... …が原因で
- ☐ COVID-19 新型コロナウイルス感染症
- ☐ outbreak 大流行
- ☐ designated 指定された
- ☐ hot-spot 高感染地域の
- ☐ prefecture 都道府県
- ☐ average 平均の
- ☐ figure 値
- ☐ mid-January 1月中旬
- ☐ mean 意味する
- ☐ commute 通う
- ☐ lack of ... …の欠如、不足

- ☐ telework 在宅勤務
- ☐ environment 環境
- ☐ failure to *do* ～しなかったこと
- ☐ on the part of ... …側の
- ☐ operate 業務を行う
- ☐ such as ... …など
- ☐ heavy 過度な
- ☐ reliance on ... …への依存
- ☐ document 文書
- ☐ stamp 刻印
- ☐ known as ... …として知られる
- ☐ approval 承認
- ☐ divide 格差
- ☐ sustain 継続する、維持する

2
- ☐ increasingly ますます
- ☐ be pressured to *do* ～するよう圧力をかけられる
- ☐ go digital デジタル化する
- ☐ as soon as possible できるだけ早く
- ☐ gap 格差
- ☐ private 私立の
- ☐ public 公立の
- ☐ evident 明らかな
- ☐ while …である一方で

- ☐ offer 提供する
- ☐ lag behind 遅れる
- ☐ moreover さらに
- ☐ remain …のままでいる
- ☐ develop 生じる
- ☐ financial 財政的な
- ☐ A as well as B Bだけでなく A も
- ☐ technical 技術的な
- ☐ nationwide 全国的に

Track 16

3 Private schools began to prepare online education platforms at the end of February when Prime Minister Shinzo Abe abruptly requested that all elementary, junior high and high schools in Japan close from March 2. Many private schools now offer educational materials such as videos and PowerPoint presentations, upload assignments and conduct teacher-student communication online.

4 The story is different when it comes to public schools. Because each student's situation is different in terms of household income and access to the internet, public schools and their municipal education boards are not asking parents to buy computers so their kids can learn online. A lack of IT-savvy teachers is another hurdle as this makes it difficult to create adequate online educational materials. Compared to other advanced nations, Japan in general has been slow to create an environment for online education.

Track 17

5 The French government closed all schools in mid-March. The government acted swiftly and started offering education programs for each grade online in the following week via the education ministry's National Center for Distance Education. The online program can also be viewed via a TV channel, so computers aren't necessary. The important thing is that the central government is taking initiatives to provide nationally standardized online materials.

3
- □ prepare 準備する
- □ platform 動作環境
- □ prime minister 首相
- □ abruptly 突然
- □ request 要請する
- □ elementary (school) 小学校
- □ junior high (school) 中学校
- □ educational material 教材
- □ presentation 提示、説明
- □ upload アップロードする→公開するためにサーバーにデータを送ることを指す
- □ assignment 課題
- □ conduct 行う

4
- □ story 事情、話
- □ when it comes to ... …に関して言えば
- □ in terms of ... …の点で
- □ household 世帯
- □ income 収入
- □ access 利用
- □ municipal 地方自治体の、市区町村の
- □ education board 教育委員会
- □ IT-savvy IT（情報技術）に詳しい
- □ hurdle 障害
- □ adequate 十分な
- □ compared to ... …に比べて
- □ advanced nation 先進国
- □ in general 概して
- □ (be) slow to *do* 〜するのが遅い

5
- □ act 行動する
- □ swiftly 素早く
- □ grade 学年
- □ following 次の
- □ via …を介して
- □ education ministry 国民教育省
- □ National Center for Distance Education 国立遠隔教育センター
- □ view 視聴する
- □ central government 中央政府
- □ take initiative 指導力を発揮する
- □ provide 提供する
- □ nationally 全国的に
- □ standardized 統一された

6   In the United States, YouTube and Google Classroom, an online educational tool developed jointly by Google and education experts, are widely used at public schools for online learning during school closures that began in March.

7   In a rare move, Japan's education ministry has finally notified its decision to the education boards across Japan that academic work done under certain conditions at home can be accepted and reflected in academic results. It also said that schools do not have to teach the same content done at home in classes once schools restart. It's good that students' work at home will be reflected academically, but this also means missed classes may not be taught by teachers. Instead, students will have to make up the classes themselves while schools are closed.

8   Parents in Japan already have enough to worry about, such as the impact of school closures on their children's physical and mental health. They may also be facing a decline in income because of the crisis. If they also have to help their children study, their burden will be even greater.

6
- YouTube ユーチューブ→米IT大手グーグル社が提供する動画共有サービス
- Google Classroom グーグルクラスルーム→グーグル社が学校向けに開発した無料のオンライン学習システムで、生徒をクラスや科目ごとに管理できる
- tool 手段、ツール
- jointly 共同で
- expert 専門家
- widely 広く
- closure 閉鎖

7
- rare まれな
- move 動き
- finally ようやく
- notify 通告する
- decision 決定
- across Japan 日本全国の
- academic work 学業
- certain 一定の
- condition 条件
- accept 認める
- reflect 反映する
- academic results 成績
- content 内容
- once いったん
- restart 再開する
- academically 学業的に
- missed 行われなかった
- instead その代わりに
- make up 補う

8
- impact 影響
- physical 身体的
- mental 精神的
- face 直面する
- decline 減少
- crisis 危機
- burden 負担
- even より一層→比較級を強める

Track 19

9 The government should not leave essential educational matters with local governments, schools and parents. Without the central government's help, disparities between private and public schools, as well as among different regions, will only become bigger. If it is not possible to provide a PC for every student at public schools due to financial and time constraints, schools should be allowed to utilize their existing facilities, such as opening up computer rooms for students who don't have online access at home.

10 If the pandemic persists for a long time, onsite schooling may not be available for weeks or months. Since opportunities to acquire education should be equally given to every child, a strong initiative on the part of the central government to shift the country's education is needed.

9
- □ leave A with B AをBに押し付ける
- □ matter 問題
- □ local government 地方自治体
- □ disparity 相違点
- □ region 地域
- □ constraint 制約
- □ allow 許す、認める
- □ utilize 活用する
- □ existing 既存の
- □ facility 設備、施設
- □ open up ... …を開放する
- □ computer room コンピュータ室

10
- □ pandemic 世界的大流行
- □ persist いつまでも続く
- □ onsite 現場での
- □ schooling 学校教育、教室授業
- □ available 利用できる
- □ for weeks 何週間もの間
- □ opportunity 機会
- □ acquire 得る
- □ shift 転換させる

Extend support for foreign students in Japan

日本にいる外国人留学生に支援の手を

April 30, 2020

●Tracks 20-25 / 訳 pp. 66-67

Track 20

1 The COVID-19 outbreak in Japan has left hundreds of thousands of university students in a chaotic situation. Lectures that were supposed to start in April only recently began to be offered online. Part-time jobs that helped students to support themselves have vanished, while the incomes of many of their parents have dwindled since the government declared the state of emergency in April.

2 A survey covering 1,200 university students released Wednesday pointed out that some 20 percent of them are considering dropping out of school as the coronavirus outbreak has left many without a source of income or financial support. The toll of this pandemic is even higher for foreign students studying in Japan.

Track 21

3 Before the spread of COVID-19, many students held part-time jobs in the restaurant and tourism industries. According to a 2019 survey on 7,000 foreign students conducted by the Japan Student Services Organization, 75.8 percent of the respondents had a part-time job, and of those, 41.8 percent worked in the restaurant sector. But those businesses are now cutting back on their operations, plunging students into a dire financial situation.

新型コロナウイルスの影響で、外国人留学生は異国の地で不安な日々を過ごしている。それは海外で学ぶ日本人留学生も同じである。意欲ある若者たちが学びの機会を奪われないようにすることは、学生だけでなくその国の将来にとっても大きな意味を持つ。

1
- ☐ [タイトル]extend 差し伸べる
- ☐ COVID-19 新型コロナウイルス感染症
- ☐ outbreak 発生、大流行
- ☐ hundreds of thousands of ... 何十万もの…
- ☐ chaotic 混沌とした
- ☐ situation 状況、事態
- ☐ be supposed to *do* 〜することになっている

- ☐ part-time job アルバイト
- ☐ support *oneself* 自活する
- ☐ vanish 消える、なくなる
- ☐ income 収入
- ☐ dwindle 減少する
- ☐ declare 宣言する
- ☐ state of emergency 緊急事態

2
- ☐ survey 調査
- ☐ cover 対象にする
- ☐ release 公表する
- ☐ point out that ... …だということを示す
- ☐ consider *doing* 〜することを考える
- ☐ drop out of school 退学する

- ☐ coronavirus コロナウイルス
- ☐ source of income 収入源
- ☐ financial 財政的な
- ☐ toll 被害、犠牲
- ☐ pandemic 世界的大流行、パンデミック

3
- ☐ spread 拡散
- ☐ tourism industry 観光業
- ☐ according to ... …によると
- ☐ conduct 実施する
- ☐ Japan Student Services Organization 日本学生支援機構
- ☐ respondent 回答者
- ☐ of those そうした人のうち→those はアルバイトをしていると回答した75.8%の人を指す

- ☐ sector 部門
- ☐ business 会社、店
- ☐ cut back on ... …を縮小する
- ☐ operation 事業
- ☐ plunge A into B AをBの状態に陥れる
- ☐ dire 差し迫った

4 It's not easy for foreign students to obtain information about government relief measures and fully understand it due to the language barrier. Living in Japan without family exacerbates psychological stress caused by the pandemic. It is extremely important to provide essential information and support to vulnerable international students.

`Track 22`

5 Recently, Japanese students at about 100 universities across the nation launched signature-collection campaigns to request that their schools reduce tuition and other expenses. So far, at least 10 universities have decided to provide some financial support for students.

6 For example, Waseda University is offering ¥100,000 for each student, while Meiji Gakuin University announced that it will provide ¥50,000. However, universities that can take such measures are limited to those with ample financial resources. Universities are still reluctant to reduce tuition fees as it would directly impact their finances.

`Track 23`

7 International students in Japan are particularly affected by job losses. Because they are students, they are not part of the unemployment insurance program. They are also not entitled to welfare benefits that are extended to low-income households. If they fail to pay their tuition and have to leave school, they will not be able to stay in Japan.

4
- ☐ obtain 入手する
- ☐ relief measure 救済措置
- ☐ fully 十分に
- ☐ due to ... …のために
- ☐ language barrier 言葉の壁
- ☐ exacerbate 悪化させる

- ☐ psychological 精神的な
- ☐ extremely 極めて
- ☐ provide 提供する
- ☐ essential 必須の
- ☐ vulnerable 弱い、影響を受けやすい

5
- ☐ across the nation 全国で
- ☐ launch 立ち上げる
- ☐ signature-collection campaign 署名運動
- ☐ request 要求する

- ☐ reduce 減らす
- ☐ tuition 授業料
- ☐ expense 費用
- ☐ so far これまでのところ

6
- ☐ announce 発表する
- ☐ be limited to ... …に限られる
- ☐ ample 豊富な
- ☐ financial resource 財源

- ☐ be reluctant to *do* 〜することに気が進まない
- ☐ fee 料金
- ☐ impact 影響を与える
- ☐ finances 財源、財政状態

7
- ☐ particularly とりわけ
- ☐ affect 影響を与える
- ☐ job loss 仕事の喪失、失業
- ☐ unemployment insurance program 雇用保険制度

- ☐ be entitled to ... …の資格がある
- ☐ welfare benefit(s) 福祉給付
- ☐ low-income household 低所得世帯
- ☐ fail to *do* 〜することができない

8　The MEXT Scholars Association has a membership of more than 8,000 current and former foreign students in Japan. According to the group's co-founder, Austin Zeng, many members have been unable to return to Japan after going back to their home countries for the spring break. Although they cannot come back to Japan, they still have to pay rent on their housing here. This is taking an especially hard toll on those who are from developing countries.

`Track 24`

9　Foreign students are eligible to receive ¥100,000 each under the government's new cash handout program, but they may find the paperwork for the funds complicated. Many of them returned to their home countries without My Number social security and taxation identification cards, which the government requires for the online application.

10　The government has long promoted a policy of increasing the number of foreign students in Japan. Young international talent tends to shun this country, and in an effort to raise the competitiveness of Japanese universities the government set a goal to raise the number of foreign students to 300,000 by 2020. Thanks to this goal, the number reached 345,791 as of the end of 2019, according to a Justice Ministry report released in late March. After such efforts by the government, the difficulties that international students are now facing should not be ignored. The government must act swiftly to make Japan a place where foreign students can safely study and live.

8
- ☐ the MEXT Scholars Association 文部科学省国費留学生協会 →MEXT はMinistry of Education, Culture, Sports, Science and Technology（文部科学省）の略
- ☐ membership 会員数
- ☐ current 現在の
- ☐ former 以前の
- ☐ co-founder 共同創設者
- ☐ be unable to *do* 〜することができない
- ☐ spring break 春休み
- ☐ rent 家賃
- ☐ housing 住宅
- ☐ take a toll on ... …に打撃を与える
- ☐ developing country 発展途上国

9
- ☐ be eligible to *do* 〜する資格がある
- ☐ cash handout 給付金
- ☐ paperwork 事務手続き
- ☐ funds 資金
- ☐ complicated 複雑な
- ☐ social security 社会保障
- ☐ taxation 課税
- ☐ identification 身元確認
- ☐ require 必要とする
- ☐ application 申請

10
- ☐ promote 推進する
- ☐ policy 政策
- ☐ increase 増やす
- ☐ tend to *do* 〜する傾向がある
- ☐ shun 避ける
- ☐ effort 取り組み
- ☐ competitiveness 競争力
- ☐ set a goal to *do* 〜するとの目標を設定する
- ☐ thanks to ... …のおかげで
- ☐ as of ... …の時点で
- ☐ Justice Ministry →法務省のこと。正式名称はthe Ministry of Justice
- ☐ difficulty 困難な状況、難題
- ☐ face 直面する
- ☐ ignore 無視する
- ☐ swiftly 迅速に

Track 25

11   The pandemic is forcing countries to close their borders, and in a crisis like this each government tends to prioritize its own citizens. Some might say that support should be extended to Japanese nationals rather than foreign students. But providing assistance to the latter is equally important for the nation's economy and its foreign relations. Young people from other countries who were given opportunities to study in Japan may become invaluable resources to shore up industries and the economy in the future. If they become fans of Japan while living here, they may become key figures to help Japan build closer relationships with their countries after they return home.

12   There are many uncertainties over how the world will look once this turbulent time is over. But one thing that is certain is that the international community is watching closely how Japan meets the needs of its foreign students.

11
- □ force ... to *do* …に〜することを余儀なくさせる
- □ border 国境
- □ crisis 危機
- □ prioritize 優先させる
- □ citizen 国民
- □ Japanese national 日本国民
- □ rather than ... …よりもむしろ
- □ assistance 援助
- □ the latter 後者→foreign students を指す
- □ equally 等しく
- □ economy 経済
- □ relation 関係
- □ opportunity 機会
- □ invaluable 計り知れない
- □ shore up ... …を支える
- □ key figure 重要な人物

12
- □ uncertainty 不確実なこと
- □ turbulent 不穏な
- □ community 共同体、社会
- □ watch closely 注視する
- □ meet the needs 必要に応える

Shore up Japan's weakened health care system

日本の弱体化した医療制度を強化する

May 7, 2020　　　　　　　　　●Tracks 26-30 / 訳 pp. 68-69

Track 26

1　As we enter the second month in a state of emergency, the COVID-19 crisis has exposed the fragility of Japan's health care system. Its capacity has been strained to the brink of breaking down amid the surge of infections and patients with grave symptoms. The government needs to learn from the current pandemic to reassess the state of the nation's medical services and rebuild their resiliency to crises.

2　Figures show that the increase in coronavirus infections nationwide is slowing—after apparently hitting a peak in mid-April—since the government declared the state of emergency a month ago. The call went out for people to maintain social distancing and stay home as much as possible, and for stores to shut down or curb their business hours. Nonetheless, experts have determined that the rate of new cases has not declined as fast as expected, and the government decided to maintain its request that social and economic activities remain curtailed through the end of May, though it left the door open to lifting the restrictions sooner if the situation is deemed to have improved.

新型コロナ危機は日本の医療制度を崩壊寸前まで追い込み、その脆弱さを暴いた。集中治療病床数は少なく、マスクと防護具は不足しており、PCR検査数も限られたままだ。新型コロナとの闘いで生き延び、かつ次の危機に備えるために、明らかになった欠点を速やかに是正すべきだ。

1
- ☐ [タイトル]shore up 支える
- ☐ [タイトル]health care system 医療制度
- ☐ state of emergency 緊急事態
- ☐ COVID-19 新型コロナウイルス感染症
- ☐ expose あらわにする
- ☐ fragility 脆弱性
- ☐ capacity 受容能力
- ☐ strain 負担をかける
- ☐ brink 瀬戸際
- ☐ surge 急増
- ☐ infection 感染症
- ☐ grave 深刻な
- ☐ symptom 症状
- ☐ pandemic (疫病の)世界的大流行
- ☐ reassess 再評価する
- ☐ resiliency 回復力

2
- ☐ figure 数値、数字
- ☐ apparently …らしい
- ☐ hit a peak 頂点に達する
- ☐ government 政府
- ☐ declare 宣言する
- ☐ call 呼び掛け、要請
- ☐ go out 伝えられる
- ☐ maintain 維持する
- ☐ social distancing 社会的距離
- ☐ as much as possible できるだけ多く
- ☐ shut down 休業する
- ☐ curb 制限する
- ☐ business hours 営業時間
- ☐ nonetheless それにもかかわらず
- ☐ expert 専門家
- ☐ case 感染者、症例
- ☐ decline 低下する、衰える
- ☐ curtail 縮小する
- ☐ leave the door open 可能性を残しておく
- ☐ lift 解除する
- ☐ restriction 制限
- ☐ situation 状況、情勢
- ☐ deem 見なす
- ☐ improve 改善する

Track 27

3 A key reason cited in maintaining the state of emergency is fear of the medical system breaking down if COVID-19 cases were to continue increasing. Even with the recent slowdown in infections, new cases still outnumber patients recovering from the illness caused by the virus. Concern that the health care system could be overwhelmed is even greater in rural parts of the country, where the infrastructure is much more fragile.

4 The number of patients with serious symptoms requiring ventilators surged over the past month—although it seemingly hit a peak in late April—and those patients require intensive care for an extended period, straining the capacity of hospitals equipped to provide such care for COVID-19 patients. A study found that Japan lags far behind other advanced economies in terms of the number of hospital beds for intensive care—around seven per 100,000 population compared with 35 in the United States, 29 in Germany and 12 in Italy—and the current situation has underlined the shortage of both medical staff and equipment to cope with a pandemic like the COVID-19 outbreak.

Track 28

5 The shortage of masks and protective gear for medical staff dealing with infectious diseases remains a serious problem. In the fight against COVID-19, more than 50 hospitals across the country have had in-house infections of doctors and nurses as well as patients. These hospitals have had to curtail their services and acceptance of new patients, putting further strain on other medical institutions in their areas.

3
- [ ] key 主な
- [ ] cite 挙げる
- [ ] fear 恐れ
- [ ] break down 崩壊する
- [ ] slowdown 鈍化
- [ ] outnumber …より多い
- [ ] patient 患者
- [ ] recover 回復する
- [ ] overwhelm 崩壊させる、圧倒する
- [ ] rural 地方の
- [ ] infrastructure インフラ、基本的施設
- [ ] fragile 脆弱な

4
- [ ] serious 深刻な
- [ ] require 必要とする
- [ ] ventilator 人工呼吸器
- [ ] surge 高まる
- [ ] seemingly 見たところ
- [ ] intensive care 集中治療
- [ ] for an extended period 長期間にわたって
- [ ] equip 必要な機能を備える
- [ ] provide 提供する
- [ ] study 調査
- [ ] lag behind 立ち遅れる
- [ ] advanced economy 先進国
- [ ] in terms of ... …の点から見て
- [ ] population 人口
- [ ] compare with ... …と比べる
- [ ] underline はっきりさせる
- [ ] shortage 不足
- [ ] equipment 設備
- [ ] cope with ... …に対処する
- [ ] outbreak （伝染病の）発生

5
- [ ] protective gear 防護具
- [ ] deal with ... …に対処する
- [ ] infectious disease 感染症、伝染病
- [ ] fight against ... …との闘い
- [ ] across the country 全国で
- [ ] in-house infection 院内感染
- [ ] acceptance 受け入れること
- [ ] further さらなる
- [ ] institution 施設
- [ ] area 地域

6   Nearly four months after the first domestic infection was confirmed, the number of PCR tests for the new coronavirus performed remains limited. As of late April, the number of tests performed per 1,000 population stood at 1.8—near the bottom among OECD member countries and far below the 29.7 in Italy, 25.1 in Germany and 11.7 in South Korea.

Track 29

7   While Prime Minister Shinzo Abe said in early April that the daily test capacity would be increased to 20,000, the number of tests performed on any single day continues to be around 8,000. Given that roughly 80 percent of the people infected with the virus develop either no or only mild symptoms, the shortage of testing underscores the persistent concern that the nation has yet to grasp the entire picture of its COVID-19 infections.

8   A panel of infectious disease experts advising the government has acknowledged that Japan failed to beef up its system for mass testing against new viruses because it did not experience heavy fallout from epidemics in recent years such as those involving SARS and MERS.

Track 30

9   Blame has been placed on the lack of manpower at local public health centers tasked with processing the PCR tests and the shortage of test kits as well as masks and protective gear. The staff at public health centers—whose numbers across the country have been nearly halved in the streamlining efforts since the 1990s— are reportedly overstretched in dealing with the current crisis.

6
- ☐ nearly ほぼ
- ☐ domestic 国内の
- ☐ confirm 確認する
- ☐ PCR test PCR検査→新型コロナウイルス感染症にかかっているかどうかを調べる検査
- ☐ perform 実施する、行う
- ☐ limited 限られた
- ☐ as of ... …現在で
- ☐ (the) bottom 最下位
- ☐ OECD 経済協力開発機構→the Organization for Economic Cooperation and Development の略
- ☐ far below ずっと下

7
- ☐ prime minister 首相
- ☐ early 上旬
- ☐ daily 毎日の
- ☐ around …ぐらい
- ☐ given that ... …を考えると
- ☐ roughly およそ、ざっと
- ☐ develop 発症する、病状が…になる
- ☐ underscore 強調する、強く示す
- ☐ persistent いつまでも残る
- ☐ concern 懸念、心配
- ☐ have yet to *do* まだ～していない
- ☐ grasp 把握する、理解する
- ☐ entire picture 全体像

8
- ☐ panel of infectious disease experts 感染症対策専門家会議
- ☐ advise 助言する
- ☐ acknowledge 認める
- ☐ fail to *do* ～しない
- ☐ beef up 強化する
- ☐ fallout 予期せぬ影響、付随的な結果
- ☐ epidemic 伝染病
- ☐ SARS 重症急性呼吸器症候群→SARSコロナウイルスによる感染症
- ☐ MERS 中東呼吸器症候群→MERSコロナウイルスによる感染症

9
- ☐ blame 責任、罪
- ☐ lack 不足
- ☐ manpower 人手
- ☐ local 地域の
- ☐ public health center 保健所
- ☐ task 仕事を課す、大きな負担をかける
- ☐ process 処理する
- ☐ halve 半減する
- ☐ streamline 合理化する
- ☐ effort 取り組み
- ☐ reportedly …と伝えられる
- ☐ overstretch 過度の要求をする

10 Crises have a way of laying bare the vulnerabilities in a society's basic infrastructure and functions. The COVID-19 pandemic is testing the resiliency of our nation's health care system, and the shortcomings exposed by this crisis must be fixed promptly, both to survive the ongoing fight against this virus—which looks set to be an extended battle even after the state of emergency is lifted—and to prepare for the next crisis.

10
- □ have a way of *doing* ～するのが普通である
- □ lay bare あらわにする、むき出しにする
- □ vulnerability 脆弱な点
- □ society 社会
- □ basic 基本的な
- □ function 機能
- □ shortcoming 欠点
- □ fix 是正する
- □ promptly すぐに
- □ survive 生き残る
- □ ongoing 進行中の
- □ look set to *do* ～しそうである
- □ extended 延長した、長い
- □ battle 闘い
- □ prepare 準備をする、備える

The state of emergency is lifted: What's next?

緊急事態宣言解除、次に取るべき方策とは

May 29, 2020　　　　　　　　　●Tracks 31-36 / 訳 pp. 70-71

Track 31

1　The government finally lifted the state of emergency in the Tokyo metropolitan area and Hokkaido earlier this week, but the battle against COVID-19 is far from over.

2　Whether in several weeks or a few months, a second coronavirus wave will likely hit Japan. To better prepare for this scenario, it is necessary to determine what measures need to be introduced now and swiftly implement them while slowly resuming economic activities.

Track 32

3　Prime Minister Shinzo Abe boasted "The Japanese model has demonstrated its strength," during a news conference on Monday in which he declared an end to the state of emergency across the country. World Health Organization Director General Tedros Adhanom Ghebreyesus called Japan's efforts to contain the epidemic a "success," saying that it has managed to reduce the spread of infection and maintain the number of COVID-19 deaths at a relatively low level. So far Japan has reported around 870 fatalities.

▼ About This Editorial ▼

安倍首相は5月25日、新型コロナウイルス対策特別措置法に基づく緊急事態宣言を全面解除した。政府は今回の感染拡大で得た教訓を生かして、検査体制の強化や困窮する事業者への資金援助を急ぎ、万全の対策をもって第2波の到来に備えるべきだ。

1
- □ [タイトル]state of emergency 緊急事態
- □ [タイトル]lift 解除する
- □ Tokyo metropolitan area 首都圏
- □ battle 闘い
- □ COVID-19 新型コロナウイルス感染症 → Corona Virus Disease 2019の略
- □ far from over 終わりには程遠い、決して終わってはいない

2
- □ whether A or B AであろうとBであろうと
- □ coronavirus コロナウイルス
- □ likely おそらく
- □ hit 襲う
- □ scenario 状況、事態
- □ determine 判断する
- □ measure(s) 対策
- □ introduce 導入する
- □ swiftly 迅速に
- □ implement 実施する
- □ resume 再開する

3
- □ prime minister 首相
- □ boast 豪語する
- □ demonstrate 実証する
- □ news conference 記者会見
- □ declare 宣言する
- □ across the country 全国で
- □ World Health Organization 世界保健機関
- □ director general 事務局長
- □ effort 取り組み
- □ contain 抑える
- □ epidemic 伝染病
- □ manage to *do* 何とかして～する
- □ reduce 減少させる
- □ spread 広がり、まん延
- □ infection 感染
- □ maintain 保つ
- □ relatively 比較的
- □ so far これまでのところ
- □ fatality 死亡者数

4 But no one is really sure what the real reason is behind the nation's success. Some say it's because Japanese people are highly health-conscious, and wash their hands and gargle frequently. Others cite a study released in May that found that countries such as Japan that require the Bacillus Calmette-Guerin (BCG) tuberculosis vaccination reported fewer COVID-19 fatalities than countries that don't. But neither explanation has been verified as a compelling reason.

Track 33

5 To better cope with a second coronavirus wave, Japan needs to build a system where more polymerase chain reaction (PCR) tests can be done. As of the end of April, the number of PCR tests per 100,000 people in Japan stood at only 188. The figure is one-sixth of South Korea and one-tenth of the United States.

6 The reason why schools and many shops had to be closed is because there is no way of knowing who is infected with the virus without sufficient PCR testing and Japan has only tested people who are highly suspected of being infected. Unless Japan raises its capacity to carry out PCR tests, there will be no means to protect its health care system other than shutting schools and businesses once again if another outbreak occurs.

Track 34

7 The Tokyo Metropolitan Government is now aiming to triple the number of testing from the end of April to 10,000 per day. Moreover, the health ministry will soon approve PCR tests using saliva instead of a throat swab. This method will slash testing times to an hour from the current six hours. Shimadzu Corp. has already confirmed that its testing kits can be used this way.

4
- ☐ behind …の背景に、裏に
- ☐ highly 非常に
- ☐ health-conscious 健康志向の
- ☐ gargle うがいをする
- ☐ frequently 頻繁に
- ☐ cite 引き合いに出す、言及する
- ☐ study 調査（結果）
- ☐ release 発表する
- ☐ find 明らかにする
- ☐ Bacillus Calmette-Guerin カルメット・ゲラン桿菌、弱毒化ウシ型結核菌
- ☐ tuberculosis 結核
- ☐ vaccination 予防接種、ワクチン接種
- ☐ neither どちらも…ない
- ☐ explanation 説明
- ☐ verify 立証する
- ☐ compelling 説得力のある

5
- ☐ cope with ... …に対処する、立ち向かう
- ☐ build 構築する
- ☐ system 制度
- ☐ polymerase chain reaction ポリメラーゼ連鎖反応
- ☐ as of ... …の時点で
- ☐ per …当たり
- ☐ stand at ... …に達する
- ☐ figure 数字
- ☐ one-sixth 6分の1
- ☐ one-tenth 10分の1

6
- ☐ close 閉鎖する
- ☐ there is no way of *doing* ～するすべがない
- ☐ be infected with ... …に感染している
- ☐ sufficient 十分な
- ☐ be suspected of ... …の疑いがある
- ☐ unless …しない限り
- ☐ raise 向上させる
- ☐ capacity 能力
- ☐ carry out 実行する
- ☐ means 手段、方策
- ☐ protect 守る
- ☐ health care system 医療体制
- ☐ shut 閉鎖する
- ☐ outbreak 大流行

7
- ☐ Tokyo Metropolitan Government 東京都
- ☐ aim to *do* ～することを目指す
- ☐ triple 3倍にする
- ☐ moreover さらに
- ☐ health ministry 厚生労働省
- ☐ approve 承認する
- ☐ saliva 唾液
- ☐ instead of ... …の代わりに
- ☐ throat swab 咽頭スワブ、咽頭拭い液
- ☐ slash （大幅に）削減する
- ☐ testing time 検査時間
- ☐ current 現在の
- ☐ Shimadzu Corp. 株式会社島津製作所
- ☐ confirm 確認する

8   The government decided to lift the state of emergency primarily because the nation's faltering economy needs to be supported. According to Teikoku Databank, the number of domestic bankruptcies this year is expected to surpass 10,000 for the first time in seven years. Meanwhile, the number of voluntary business closures that are not officially categorized as bankruptcies is likely to reach 25,000.

Track 35

9   On Wednesday, the Cabinet approved a second supplementary budget totaling ¥31.9 trillion to enable another relief package worth over ¥100 trillion. It is commendable that the package includes financial support to cover from one-third to two-thirds of business operators' rent up to ¥6 million, among many other measures. But it must be noted that the government policies announced earlier, such as providing ¥100,000 for every individual and subsidies to support shops and bars that voluntarily closed, have yet to be fully implemented.

10   Following the 2008 global financial crisis, there was a spike in bankruptcies among manufacturers. This time a sharp decline in foreign tourists severely affected the hotel and the tourism industries, while the state of emergency inflicted tremendous financial damage on restaurants and bar operators. The transportation industry is expected to be impacted next. As more companies encourage employees to work from home, demand for office space in urban areas is also likely to drop sharply, which will affect the real estate industry. Many other industries are likely to suffer as well.

8
- [ ] primarily 主に
- [ ] faltering 低迷している
- [ ] according to ... …によると
- [ ] Teikoku Databank 帝国データバンク
- [ ] domestic 国内の
- [ ] bankruptcy 倒産
- [ ] be expected to *do* 〜すると予想される
- [ ] surpass 超える
- [ ] for the first time 初めて
- [ ] meanwhile 一方で
- [ ] voluntary 自主的な
- [ ] closure 休廃業
- [ ] officially 正式に
- [ ] categorize 分類する

9
- [ ] Cabinet 内閣
- [ ] supplementary budget 追加［補正］予算
- [ ] total 合計で…になる
- [ ] trillion 1兆
- [ ] enable 可能にする
- [ ] relief package （一連の）救済措置
- [ ] worth （金額が）…相当の
- [ ] commendable 評価できる
- [ ] cover …を対象とする
- [ ] business operator 事業者
- [ ] rent 家賃、賃貸料
- [ ] up to ... 最大…まで
- [ ] among …の中で
- [ ] note 留意する
- [ ] individual 個人
- [ ] subsidy 補助金
- [ ] voluntarily 自発的に
- [ ] yet to *do* まだ〜されていない
- [ ] fully 完全に

10
- [ ] following …に続いて
- [ ] financial crisis 金融危機
- [ ] spike 急増
- [ ] manufacturer 製造業者
- [ ] sharp 急激な
- [ ] decline 減少
- [ ] foreign tourist 海外からの観光客
- [ ] severely ひどく
- [ ] affect 影響を与える
- [ ] industry 業界
- [ ] inflict 与える
- [ ] tremendous 多大な
- [ ] financial damage 財政的打撃
- [ ] transportation 運輸
- [ ] impact 影響を与える
- [ ] encourage 奨励する
- [ ] employee 従業員
- [ ] demand 需要
- [ ] urban 都会の
- [ ] drop 減少する
- [ ] real estate 不動産
- [ ] suffer 損害を被る

Track 36

11 Unless the government's financial support reaches those who are in need, there will be more bankruptcies and more people out of work. The government must make an effort to make the paperwork process as smooth as possible and quickly offer financial aid to businesses that need it.

12 Different phases of the pandemic require different policy measures. The government and health officials should utilize the lessons they learned in the first phase of the epidemic. If they can prepare better for the second wave of COVID-19, it will be possible to avoid a second state of emergency.

11
- □ in need 困窮している
- □ out of work 失業して、無職の
- □ make an effort 努力する
- □ paperwork process 事務手続き
- □ as ... as possible できるだけ…に
- □ smooth 円滑な
- □ quickly 迅速に
- □ offer 提供する
- □ financial aid 資金援助

12
- □ different 異なる
- □ phase 段階
- □ pandemic（疫病の）世界的大流行
- □ policy measure(s) 政策措置
- □ official 当局者
- □ utilize 生かす
- □ lesson 教訓
- □ possible 可能性がある
- □ avoid 回避する

新型コロナウイルス感染症による医療崩壊を防ぐ

1 政府に提言を行っている感染症対策専門家会議によると、新型コロナウイルス感染症（COVID-19）の国内感染急増を阻止する取り組みにおいて、日本は今後1、2週間、重大な岐路に置かれる。しかし、今週初めに発表された政府の基本方針（原則的に厚労省がすでに発表した指針に沿っている）は、その危機感を共有しているようには見えない。COVID-19の国内発生を封じ込める取り組みは、大量感染の重圧で国の医療システムが崩壊するという最悪のシナリオを想定し、それを回避する処置を講じることによってより迅速化できる。

2 COVID-19との闘いの焦点は、国境を越える感染の予防から、大規模な国内発生を食い止めることに移った。ある専門家委員会は、現在の優先事項は、新しい感染の増加を抑制し、死につながる可能性のある重篤な症状を発症する人の数を最小限に抑えることだと述べている。その専門家委員会は、感染した個々人によって知らないうちに集団感染が広がる可能性について警告し、多数の人と長時間にわたって濃厚接触するような集会やイベントに出席することを控えるよう、すべての人々に要請している。

3 しかし、火曜日に発表された基本方針で、政府は、そのようなイベントを中止・延期するよう主催者に一律に求めることはせず、（経済活動を妨げることへの政府の抵抗感を反映していると報じられる表現で）集会の必要性を再検討するよう求めると述べた。だが、安倍晋三首相は水曜日に、政府はこれから、多数の参加者が関わるスポーツや文化イベントを、今後2週間は中止、延期、または規模縮小するよう要請していくと語った。

4 （最初に感染が発生した）中国への最近の渡航歴がない人々の感染が急増していることを考えると、今後の主要な課題は、COVID-19やその他の患者を治療する医療サービスの崩壊を防ぐことだ。

5 これまでのところ、新型コロナウイルスに感染した人々は、ウイルスの流出を防ぐための気密施設を備えた感染症指定病院で手当てを受けている。しかし、首都圏にあるそれらの医療機関の多くが、現在、クルーズ船ダイヤモンド・プリンセス乗船中に感染した数百人の患者で埋まっており、肺炎を発症したCOVID-19の患者の治療に必要な人工呼吸器の不足に対する懸念が高まっている。このような状況下での集団感染の拡大は、そうした医療機関の崩壊を引き起こし、通常の状況な

ら命を救うことができるであろう患者（ほかの病気にかかっている人々を含む）を危機にさらすだろうと述べる警告が出されている。

6 政府の基本方針によれば、COVID-19の患者数が急激に増加した地域では、感染症患者の治療に指定されていない病院も、コロナウイルス感染の可能性のある人々を、ほかの患者から隔離するという条件で受け入れるよう求められている。国内の多くの地域の非指定病院が、このような条件でCOVID-19の患者を受け入れる準備がないことを、複数の報道が示している。そのような患者を安全に受け入れるのに必要な措置が取れ、感染した可能性がある多数の人々が少数の病院に集中することを避けることができるよう、こうした病院のための指針を確立する取り組みを促進しなければならない。

7 COVID-19の拡大を防ぐ上で、すべての人々が役割を担っている。感染したかもしれない恐れがあっても重篤な症状のない人は、医療機関に行くのを控えるべきだ。もし行けば、実際に病気にかかっている人が必要とする貴重な医療資源を使ったり、また、病気をさらに広めるリスクを高めたりすることになる。感染症専門家は医療機関が集団感染の培養器になり得ると警告している。軽い、風邪に似た症状がある人々が、病院に行かずに自宅にいて確実に安全だと感じられるように、基本方針が求める通りに、政府は具体的な措置を導入しなければならない。

8 今回の疫病の流行に対する人々の不安感を和らげる一つの方法は、（供給が限られている）COVID-19のウイルス検査を受診しやすくすることだ。これにより、より多くの人々が検査を受け、知らないうちに病気を広めるのを止めることができる。加藤勝信厚労相は水曜日の国会で、直近の1週間に、平均しておよそ900件の新型ウイルスに対する検査が毎日行われたと述べた。これは、政府が以前に可能だと述べた一日最大3,800件をはるかに下回っている。関係当局は、ウイルス検査の供給増加を妨げる諸問題を解決して、検査を望むすべての人々が利用できるように民間部門の資源の使用拡大を含めて措置を講じるべきだ。（訳・注 中村）

2021年東京五輪開催に向けた課題

1　東京オリンピック・パラリンピックが2021年夏までの最長1年間延期されたことは、世界を席巻しているコロナウイルスの世界的大流行を踏まえればやむを得ないことだったが、参加選手全員の公平性を確保すると望まれる合理的な決断だ。これからは、選手のみならず世界中から訪れるであろうすべての大会関係者や観客にとっても安全な環境で、大会を来年開催することに取り組みを移すべきだ。

2　国際オリンピック委員会（IOC）は、大会を予定通り進めるとつい先週発表したものの、それが不可能であることはますます明らかになってきていた。世界中で新型コロナウイルス感染症（COVID-19）の感染者数は今週40万人を超え（わずか1週間前の2倍）、2万人超が死亡した。世界的流行が7月までに収束して、日本が国内でのまん延をどうにか抑えられたとしても、膨大な数の観客を大会に迎え入れられる見通しはなかった。延期の決定を受けて世界保健機関（WHO）は、2020年の大会を進めていたら大流行をさらに深刻化させる結果になっていただろうと日本とIOCに警告していたことを明らかにした。

3　世界中の選手や競技団体からIOCに対して大会延期への圧力が高まり、一部の国のオリンピック委員会は、予定通り7月に大会が開始されるのなら自国の選手を東京に派遣しないと述べていた。今回の感染症の世界的大流行は、選手らから最高のコンディションで五輪に備える機会を奪った。ほかの主要な国際競技大会は取りやめとなり、予選大会の中止により東京五輪出場枠約1万1,000人のうち40%を超える数の選考が実施されていないままとなっている。五輪をこの夏に開くのは、多くの選手から公平な競争条件を奪うことになるため不公平なものとなったであろう。

4　とはいうものの、開催日程変更というかつてない作業は実にさまざまな難題を伴うこととなる（124年の五輪史上、中止は5回あったが、東京で開催される予定だった1940年の五輪を含めいずれも戦争が理由だった）。その筆頭にあるのは、来年の大会開催までにCOVID-19の大流行を確実に抑え込むことだが、それが達成できる保証はまったくない。世界各地からやってくる選手、スポーツ関係者、観客など関わる人々全員の安全確保が、引き続き大会運営の優先事項となるだろう。

5　課題は、来年開催が予定されているほかの国際競技大会の日程調整から、2021年五輪の各種目の会場確保、参加者の宿泊先や移動手段の再調整、競技運営に携わるボランティア数万人の再編まで多岐にわたる。

6　開催の延期によって選考過程のやり直しが必要となれば、大会参加選手を選ぶ際の公平性の確保も重要だ。五輪の延期には数千億円もの巨額の追加費用がかかると予想されている。どこが、そしてどのように、それを負担するのか、早急に決定しなければならない。

7　大会延期はオリンピック関連の経済的利益を先送りする。訪日観光客の激減など疫病大流行の影響ですでに打撃を受け、長期不況に突入するという懸念が広まっている日本経済にとって、このことはさらなる悩みの種となるだろう。政府は、延期が発表されたときにちょうど「感染拡大の重大局面にある」とされた東京をはじめ、国内でのCOVID-19感染拡大と闘いながら、経済的損失を抑制する対策を講じなければならない。

8　2020年の五輪開催を自身の長期政権の重要な遺産にしたいと考えてきた安倍晋三首相が、大会を一年延期することを主導したと見られている。IOCが正式に五輪開催の延期を決定するに先立って、安倍首相とトーマス・バッハIOC会長の間でその旨の合意がなされたが、それはIOCが結論を4週間以内に出すと発表したわずか2日後のことだった。大会中止という最悪の事態よりは、延期のほうがましな選択肢であることは確かだ。今回の決断が来年の五輪開催の成功につながるかどうかは、日本が今後数カ月で何を達成できるかに大いにかかっている。

（訳・注 宇都宮）

今がコロナウイルス危機を抑え込めるかどうかの正念場

1 われわれは、東京とそれ以外の6道府県でコロナウイルス感染者数の急増を理由に今週政府から出された緊急事態宣言によって、パニックに陥るのではなく、事態を深刻に受け取るべきである。新型コロナウイルス感染症（COVID-19）の大流行を抑え込めるかどうかはひとえにわれわれ一人一人の行動にかかっている。一方、政府の側は、国全体が感染症の世界的大流行と闘う中、失業や収入減に苦しんでいる人々の生活を守るセーフティーネット（救済策）を確実に用意しておく必要がある。

2 より大規模な感染の流行が発生している国々の多くの大都市で課されているロックダウン（地域封鎖）とは異なり、5月6日まで続く日本の緊急事態宣言には、指定された地域の人々に対して、不可欠あるいは緊急の用事がある場合を除いて、自宅にとどまるようにという政府の要請に従わないことに対する罰則は存在しない。このような措置が増大するコロナウイルスの流行を効果的に抑えることができるかどうかは、国民一人一人がどのような対応を取るかに大きくかかっている。

3 政府は複数の専門家の提言を引用し、国民に人との接触を最低でも7割から8割減らすように要請している。これは、数週間以内に感染率が最高点に達し、その後減少へとつながることが望まれる行動である。これがどれほど早く達成できるかはわれわれの行動次第である。

4 伝えられるところによると、全世界にまん延しているパンデミックという重圧の下、すでに景気後退に向かいつつあったわが国の経済にさらなる悪影響を及ぼすことを避けるために、安倍政権は緊急事態宣言を出すことを何週間もためらってきたという。今回の措置は、国民や企業がその活動を自粛するため、確実に日本経済に深刻な打撃を与えることになる。

5 緊急事態宣言の発令に加え、安倍政権はパンデミックによって引き起こされる経済的打撃を緩和するため、108兆円に上る一連の経済政策を取った。これは史上最大規模のものだと喧伝されており、実際、2008年のリーマン・ブラザーズの破綻に続く世界規模の金融危機のさなかに導入された56兆円の景気刺激策の2倍近い規模のものとなる。ただ、その一連の政策のとてつもない（政府の2020年会計年度の年間予算をも上回る）規模自体はさておき、最も深刻な打撃を受けた

人々、すなわちこのパンデミックにおいて仕事や収入を失う人々に十分な支援が
確実に提供されるために、その実際の中身が精査される必要がある。

6 ウイルスとの闘いにおいて国民の協力を確実に得るためには、特にその闘いが今
後どれだけ続くかが相変わらず不確定であるため、国民の生活を守るための信頼
できるセーフティーネットが不可欠となるだろう。今回の一連の経済政策はそれが
支援を本当に必要としている人々の助けとなっているかどうかを見極めるため、見
直しや更新を図っていく必要がある。

7 主要な優先事項は、パンデミックによってすでに瀬戸際に追い込まれてきている
医療体制の崩壊を食い止めることである。日本で確認された感染者数や死者の数
は、何十万人もの人々が感染し、1万人超が亡くなっている米国、イタリア、フラ
ンスやスペインといった国々よりはずっと少ないかもしれない。ただここ数日で急
激に加速している感染者数の増加のペース、とりわけ感染経路が不明の患者数の
急増が、医療サービスの崩壊を引き起こしかねない感染の爆発的増加が起きる可
能性について警鐘を鳴らしている。

8 過度な負荷のかかった医療システムが重篤な症状を抱える人々に適時に治療を施
すことができなくなる事態は避けなければならない。今週、東京都の当局は医療
機関がその限られた資源をより重い症状の患者に集中させることができるように、
軽症あるいは無症状のCOVID-19感染者をホテルに移す措置を取り始めた。ただ、何としても避けなければならないのは感染者の爆発的な増加で、そうしたこ
とが起きれば、COVID-19の患者のみならず、ほかの深刻な病気を抱えた患者が
必要な医療支援を受けられなくなってしまう。

9 わが国が、経済や国民の生活への打撃を食い止める一方で、感染の拡大を抑え込
み、そうした大惨事をうまく避けることができるかどうかはわれわれ自身が今すぐ
行う取り組みに大きくかかっている。政府はこうした努力を支えるために、十分な
支援を提供しなければならない。このことは、長期的な危機となるかもしれない
事態への政府の対応に関して国民の信頼を勝ち取るために不可欠となる。

（訳・注　小川）

新型コロナ休校中、国の支援が不可欠

1　4月7日に新型コロナウイルス感染症（COVID-19）の流行による緊急事態宣言が発令されてから1週間以上がたつ。だが、誰もが外出を自粛しているわけではないようだ。政府が発表したデータによると、対象とされた感染中心地である7都府県で、主要駅周辺の月曜日の人出は（感染拡大前の）1月中旬から1カ月間の平均値と比べて40％から60％の減少となった。これが意味しているのは、自宅に在宅勤務の環境が整っていない、あるいは勤務先側が紙文書への過度な依存や、その内容承認のためのハンコと呼ばれる昔ながらの刻印の使用といった従来の仕事のやり方を変えていないことが理由で、まだ通勤している人がいるということだ。こういった状況が、オンラインで事業を継続できる企業とそうでない企業の間に大きな格差を生んでいる。

2　全国の学校にも、できるだけ早くデジタル化を進めるようますます圧力がかかっている。対象の7都府県ではほとんどの学校が5月6日まで休校となっているため、私立と公立校の格差がより顕著になってきた。私立の多くが今月からオンライン学習プログラムを提供し始めた一方で、公立は大きく後れを取っている。さらに、対象外の地域の学校が開校し続ければ休校の学校との間に差が生じる。政府は全国の学校にデジタル化のための技術支援だけでなく資金援助も行うべきだ。

3　私立校がオンライン教育プラットフォームを準備し始めたのは2月末、安倍晋三首相が突然、全国の小中学校および高校に3月2日からの一斉休校を要請したときだ。現在、私立校の多くは動画やパワーポイントでの説明といった教材の提供や、課題のアップロード、教師と生徒間のやりとりをオンラインで行っている。

4　これが公立校となると話は違ってくる。世帯収入やインターネットへのアクセス状況は生徒によって異なるため、公立校やそれを管理する市区町村の教育委員会は保護者に対して、子どものオンライン学習のためにコンピュータを購入するよう求めてはいない。もう一つの障害はITに詳しい教師の不足で、このことが適切なオンライン教材の作成を困難にしている。ほかの先進国に比べ、日本は概してオンライン教育の環境整備が遅れている。

5　フランス政府は3月中旬にすべての学校を休校にした。政府は迅速に対応し、その翌週には国民教育省の国立遠隔教育センターを通じて学年ごとの教育プログラムをオンラインで提供し始めた。このオンライン・プログラムの視聴はテレビの

チャンネル経由でも可能なので、コンピュータが必要ではない。重要なのは、中央政府が率先して全国共通のオンライン教材を提供していることだ。

6 米国では「ユーチューブ」そして、グーグル社と教育専門家が共同開発したオンライン教育ツール「グーグルクラスルーム」が、3月に始まった学校閉鎖の期間中、オンライン学習のために公立校で広く使われている。

7 めったにない動きだが、日本の文科省は全国の教育委員会に対してようやく、一定の条件下で行われる家庭学習を認め、それを成績に反映させることができるという決定を通知した。また、学校再開後に、家庭で学習したことと同じ内容を授業で教える必要はないとしている。生徒の家庭学習が成績に反映されるのはよいことだが、これはまた、実施されなかった授業の内容は教師が教えない可能性があるということを意味する。その代わりに生徒が休校中の授業を自分で補わなければならない。

8 休校が子どもたちの心身の健康に与える影響など、日本の保護者にはすでに心配なことがたくさんある。また、今回の危機で収入の減少という問題に直面しているかもしれない。子どもたちが勉強するのも手伝わなければならないとなると、負担はさらに大きくなる。

9 政府は重要な教育問題を地方自治体や学校、保護者に任せっぱなしにすべきではない。国の支援なしでは地域差はもちろん、私立校と公立校の格差は広がるばかりだ。経済的・時間的な制約で公立の全生徒にパソコンを提供できないのなら、家庭でインターネットが利用できない生徒にコンピュータ室を開放するなど、学校に既存施設の活用を認めるべきだ。

10 新型コロナウイルスの世界的大流行が長引けば数週間から数カ月間、教室での授業が受けられない可能性がある。教育を受ける機会はすべての子どもに平等に与えられるべきなので、日本の教育を転換させるために中央政府としての強い指導力を発揮することが必要だ。　　　　　　　　　　　　　　　　　（訳・注　宇都宮）

日本にいる外国人留学生に支援の手を

1　日本での新型コロナウイルス感染症（COVID-19）の大流行は、何十万人もの大学生を混沌とした状況に追い込んだ。4月に開始予定だった講義は、最近になってようやくオンラインで提供され始めた。学生たちが自活するのを支えていたアルバイトはなくなる一方、4月に政府が緊急事態を宣言して以降、彼らの親たちの多くの収入も減少した。

2　水曜日に公表された1,200人の大学生を対象とした調査では、そのうちの約20%が退学を考えているということを示しているが、それはコロナウイルスの流行で多くの大学生が収入源や財政的な支援のない状態にされたためだ。今回の感染症の世界的大流行（パンデミック）の打撃は、日本で学ぶ外国人留学生たちにとってはさらに大きい。

3　COVID−19の拡散前、多くの学生たちは飲食業や観光業でアルバイトをしていた。日本学生支援機構が7,000人の外国人留学生を対象に実施した2019年の調査によると、回答者の75.8%がアルバイトをしていて、そのうちの41.8%が飲食業部門で働いていた。しかし、これらの店は現在、事業を縮小しており、そのため、学生たちを厳しい経済状況に陥れている。

4　外国人留学生たちが政府の救済措置に関する情報を入手し、それを完全に理解することは、言葉の壁のために容易ではない。家族と離れて日本で暮らすことは、今回のパンデミックによって引き起こされた精神的なストレスを悪化させる。弱い立場にある留学生たちに対して、必須の情報と支援を提供することが極めて重要である。

5　先ごろ、日本全国の100余りの大学の日本人学生たちが、学校側に対して授業料などの費用を引き下げるように要求する署名運動を立ち上げた。これまでのところ、少なくとも10の大学が学生に向けて何らかの財政支援を提供すると決定した。

6　たとえば、早稲田大学は学生一人当たり10万円を支給する一方、明治学院大学は5万円を提供すると発表した。けれども、そのような対策を実施できる大学は、豊富な財源があるところに限られる。財政状態に直接の影響を及ぼすことから、大学はいまだに授業料の削減に前向きではない。

7　日本にいる留学生たちは、働き口の喪失によってとりわけ打撃を受けている。彼

らは学生であるため、雇用保険制度の加入対象ではない。また、低所得世帯に渡される福祉給付を受ける資格もない。授業料を支払えず、大学をやめなければならないとしたら、日本に滞在することができなくなるであろう。

8 文部科学省国費留学生協会には、現役およびかつての日本の外国人留学生8,000人超の会員がいる。協会の共同創設者オースティン・ゼン氏によると、多くの会員たちは春休みで母国に戻ったあと、日本に帰って来られずにいるという。日本に戻れないにもかかわらず、それでも彼らは日本での住宅の家賃を支払わなければならない。このことは発展途上国出身の学生たちにとって、とりわけ厳しい打撃になっている。

9 外国人留学生たちは政府による新たな給付金制度の下で、それぞれ10万円を受ける資格があるが、資金のための事務手続きを複雑だと感じるかもしれない。彼らの多くは、政府がオンライン申請の際に求める社会保障と課税の身元確認カードであるマイナンバーカードがないまま母国に帰国した。

10 政府は長年にわたって日本の外国人留学生の人数を増やす政策を推進してきた。世界各国の若い才能の持ち主たちはこの国を避ける傾向があり、日本の大学の競争力を高める取り組みとして、政府は外国人留学生の人数を2020年までに30万人に増加させるとの目標を設定した。この目標のおかげで、法務省が3月の終わりに公表した報告書によると、2019年末の時点でその数は34万5,791人に達した。政府がそうした取り組みを行ったのだから、留学生たちが現在直面している困難な状況は無視されるべきではない。日本を外国人留学生たちが安心して学んで暮らせる場所にするために、政府は迅速に行動しなければならない。

11 パンデミックのために各国は国境の封鎖を余儀なくされているし、このような危機に際して各国政府は自国民を最優先に考えがちである。支援は外国人留学生よりもむしろ日本国民に向けられるべきだと言う人もいるかもしれない。しかし、留学生たちに対して援助を提供することも、国の経済および外国との関係にとっては等しく重要である。日本で学ぶ機会を与えられたほかの国からの若者たちが、将来に産業と経済を支える計り知れない価値を持つ人材となるかもしれない。この国で生活している間に日本のファンになれば、帰国したあと、日本がその国とより緊密な関係を築くのを助ける重要な人物になるかもしれない。

12 この不穏な日々が終わりを迎えたとき、世界がどうなっているのかについては多くの不確定要素がある。しかし、一つはっきりと言えるのは、日本が外国人留学生の必要にどう応えるか、国際社会が注視しているという点である。（訳・注　桑田）

日本の弱体化した医療制度を強化する

1 緊急事態の２カ月目に入り、新型コロナウイルス感染症（COVID-19）の危機は、日本の医療制度の脆弱さを露呈している。感染と重症患者が急増する中、受け入れ能力は崩壊瀬戸際まで追い詰められた。政府は、国の医療サービスの実態を再評価し、危機に対する回復力を再構築するために、現在の感染症の世界的大流行（パンデミック）から学ぶ必要がある。

2 政府が１カ月前に緊急事態を宣言して以来、全国的なコロナウイルス感染拡大が（おそらく４月中旬に頂点に達した後に）鈍ってきたことを、数値が示している。人々に対しては、社会的距離を保ってできるだけ外出しないよう、また、商店に対しては、休業するか営業時間を短縮するよう、呼び掛けられた。それでも、専門家たちは新規感染率が予想ほど早くは下がっていないと判断し、政府は、状況が改善したと見なされたら早めに制限を解除するという選択肢も残しておきつつ、引き続き社会・経済活動を５月末まで抑えるという要請を維持する決断をした。

3 緊急事態措置を維持する主な理由として挙げられたのが、COVID-19の感染者数が増加し続けた場合に医療制度が崩壊する恐れである。このところ感染は減速しているが、新規感染者数は依然として、新型コロナウイルスによる感染症から回復する患者の数を上回っている。医療制度が崩壊するかもしれないという懸念は、インフラがより一層脆弱であるこの国の地方部では、さらに大きい。

4 人工呼吸器を必要とする重症患者の数は（４月下旬に天井を打ったと見られるものの）過去１カ月間に膨れ上がり、これらの患者が長期間の集中治療を必要とするため、COVID-19の患者にそうした治療を提供する設備がある病院の治療能力に負担をかけている。ある調査によると、日本は病院の集中治療病床数において、ほかの先進国に大きく後れを取っており（人口10万人に付きおよそ７人で、それに比べ米国は35人、ドイツは29人、イタリアは12人である）、現在の状況は、COVID-19発生のようなパンデミックに対処する医療スタッフと機器の両方の不足を浮き彫りにしている。

5 感染症に対処する医療スタッフのためのマスクと防護具の不足も相変わらず深刻な問題だ。COVID-19との闘いにおいて、全国50軒を超える病院で、医師、看護師および患者の院内感染が発生している。これらの病院は医療活動と新患受け入れを縮小せざるを得なくなり、地域のほかの医療機関にさらなる負担がかかっている。

6 最初の国内感染が確認されてから4カ月近くが過ぎたが、新型コロナウイルスのPCR検査数はいまだに限られている。4月下旬の時点で、実施された検査数は人口1,000人当たり1.8人だった（これはOECD加盟国中最下位に近く、イタリアの29.7人、ドイツの25.1人、韓国の11.7人をはるかに下回る）。

7 安倍晋三首相は4月上旬、毎日の検査能力を2万件に増やすと述べたが、どの一日をとっても日々の検査実施数は依然として8,000件前後のままである。ウイルスに感染した人々のおよそ80%の病状が無症状、または軽症であることを考慮すれば、検査不足は、日本がいまだにCOVID-19の感染の全体像を把握するに至っていないという根強い懸念を強めるものである。

8 政府に助言する感染症対策専門家会議は、日本が近年SARSやMERSに関わる伝染病の深刻な影響を経験しなかったため、新型ウイルスに対する大量検査制度を強化するのを怠ったと認めている。

9 PCR検査の処理を担当する地域の保健所の人員不足と、検査キット、さらにはマスク、防護具の不足が原因だと非難されている。伝えられるところによれば、保健所の職員（1990年代以降、合理化の取り組みで全国の職員数がほぼ半減した）は、目下の危機に対処するため無理をさせられているという。

10 危機とは、社会の基本的なインフラと機能の脆弱な点をさらけ出すものである。COVID-19のパンデミックはわが国の医療制度の回復力を試練にかけているが、この危機によって露呈した欠点は、進行中の（緊急事態解除後も延長戦になりそうな）対ウイルス戦で生き残るため、また、次の危機に備えるために、速やかに是正すべきである。　　　　　　　　　　　　　　　　　　　（訳・注　中村）

緊急事態宣言解除、次に取るべき方策とは

1 政府は今週初め、首都圏と北海道における緊急事態宣言をようやく解除したが、新型コロナウイルス感染症（COVID-19）との闘いは決して終わってはいない。

2 数週間後であろうと、数カ月後であろうと、新型コロナウイルスの第2波が日本に到来する可能性は高い。そうした事態に一層周到に備えるためには、今どのような対策を導入する必要があるのかを見極め、経済活動を徐々に再開しながらそうした対策を速やかに実施することが必要だ。

3 安倍晋三首相は月曜日の記者会見で緊急事態宣言の全面解除を表明した際、「日本モデルがその強さを実証した」と自慢げに話した。世界保健機関（WHO）のテドロス・アダノム・ゲブレイェソス事務局長は、日本は首尾よく感染拡大を抑えてCOVID-19による死者数を比較的低い水準に維持してきたと述べ、流行を抑え込もうとする日本の取り組みを「成功」と呼んだ。これまでのところ、日本ではおよそ870人の死亡が報告されている。

4 だがこの国の成功の本当の理由が何なのかは、誰もはっきりとはわかっていない。日本人は健康意識が非常に高く、手洗いとうがいをこまめにしているからだという人がいる。また、日本のようにBCG接種が義務化されている国ではそうでない国に比べてCOVID-19による死亡の報告件数が少ないとする、5月に発表された調査結果を引き合いに出す人もいる。しかし、どちらの説明も有力な根拠として立証されていない。

5 新型コロナウイルスの第2波によりうまく立ち向かうため、日本はさらに多くのPCR検査を実施できる制度を構築する必要がある。4月末の時点で、日本における人口10万人当たりのPCR検査件数はわずか188件だった。その数は韓国の6分の1、米国の10分の1である。

6 学校や多数の店舗が閉鎖せざるを得なかったのは、十分なPCR検査なしには誰がウイルスに感染しているかを知るすべがなく、日本では感染の疑いが強い人にしか検査が行われてこなかったからだ。日本はPCR検査能力を向上させない限り、もう一度感染が広がれば、学校や企業を再び閉鎖する以外に医療体制を守る手段はないだろう。

7 東京都は現在、一日当たりの検査回数を4月末の3倍となる1万件に増やすことを目指している。さらに厚生労働省は近く、咽頭スワブの代わりに唾液を使ったPCR検査を認可する予定だ。この方法で検査時間は現在の6時間から1時間に大幅に短縮される。島津製作所はすでに自社の検査キットがこの方法に使えることを確認している。

8 政府が緊急事態宣言解除に踏み切った主な理由は、低迷する景気を下支えしなければならないことだ。帝国データバンクによると、国内企業の倒産件数は今年7年ぶりに1万件を超える見通しだ。一方、正式には倒産に分類されない自主廃業は2万5,000件に達する見込みだ。

9 水曜日に内閣は、100兆円超規模の一連の追加救済対策を可能にする総額31兆9000億円の第2次補正予算案を閣議決定した。その多くの対策の中でも特に、事業者の家賃の3分の1から3分の2、最大600万円を支給する資金援助を盛り込んだことは評価できる。ただ、すべての国民一人当たり10万円の支給や自主休業をした店やバーを支援する補助金など、政府が以前に発表した政策はまだ完全に実施されていないことに留意すべきだ。

10 2008年の世界的金融危機後、製造業者の倒産が急増した。今回は外国人観光客の激減がホテル・観光業界に深刻な経済的影響をもたらす一方で、緊急事態宣言がレストランやバーの経営者に多大な損害を与えた。次に影響を受けるのは運輸業界だと予想されている。在宅勤務を奨励する企業が増えるにつれて、都市部のオフィス用スペースの需要も大幅に減少する可能性が高く、それが不動産業界に影響を及ぼすだろう。ほかの多くの産業も同じく損害を被ることになりそうだ。

11 政府の経済的支援が困窮者に届かなければ、倒産や失業者がさらに増えるだろう。政府はできる限り事務手続きの円滑化を図り、支援が必要な事業者への迅速な資金援助提供に努めなければならない。

12 パンデミックの段階が変われば、政策措置も違ったものが必要になる。政府と保健当局は、流行の第1段階で得た教訓を生かすべきだ。COVID-19の第2波に対してもっとしっかりと備えることができれば、2度目の緊急事態宣言を回避することができるだろう。

（訳・注　宇都宮）

WILL 'FLU' COME BACK?

スペイン風邪は再来するのか

Thursday, October 23, 1919

Track 37

1   "Will the 'flu' come back this year?" a question being asked by thousands of scientists and millions of laymen throughout the world is discussed in an official bulletin in Washington, in which it is said that the plague probably will reappear but not as severe as last winter. One authority says "Indications are, that should it occur, it will not be as severe as the pandemic of the previous year." City officials, state and city boards of health, should be prepared in the event of a recurrence. The fact that a previous attack brings immunity in a certain percentage of cases should allay fear on the part of those afflicted in the previous epidemic.

2   Influenza is spread by direct and indirect contact. It is not yet certain that the germ has been isolated, or discovered, so as a consequence there is yet no positive preventive, except the enforcement of rigid rules of sanitation and the avoidance of personal contact. A close relation between the influenza pandemic and the constantly increasing pneumonia mortality rate prior to the fall of 1918 is recognized. It is now believed that the disease was pretty widely disseminated before it was recognized in its

---

1 □［タイトル］(the) flu インフルエンザ、流感→influenzaを短くした語□ layman 素人□ throughout the world 世界中□ official bulletin 公報□ plague 伝染病、疫病□ reappear 再発する □ severe 深刻な□ authority 権威、当局□ indication 兆候□ occur 発生する、起きる□ pandemic（疫病の）世界的流行□ previous 前の□ board of health 衛生局□ be prepared 備えている□ in the event of ... …の場合には□ recurrence 再発□ immunity 免疫□ allay 和らげる□ on the part of ... …の側の□ afflict 苦しめる□ epidemic 伝染病

2 □ spread 広がる、拡散する→過去形・過去分詞形も spread□ indirect 間接的な□ contact 接触□ germ 病原菌□ isolate 分離する□ as a consequence 結果として□ positive 確かな□ preventive 予防策□ enforcement 施行□ rigid 厳格な□ sanitation 衛生□ avoidance 回避、避けること□ constantly 絶えず□ pneumonia 肺炎□ mortality rate 死亡率□ prior to ... …より前の□

epidemic state. This failure to recognize the early cases appears to have largely been due to the fact that every interest was then centered on the war.

Track 38

3 Concerning the important question of immunity conferred by an attack of influenza, the evidence is not conclusive, but there is reason to believe that an attack during the earlier stages of the epidemic confers a considerable, but not absolute immunity in the later outbreaks.

4 Despite the fact that there is still some uncertainty as to the nature of the micro-organism causing influenza, one thing is certain, that the disease is communicable from person to person. Moreover, judging from experience in other diseases, it is probable that the germ, whatever its nature, is carried about not only by those who are ill with influenza, but by persons who may be entirely well. Everything which increases personal contact, therefore, should be regarded as a factor in spreading influenza.

---

recognize 認める□disseminate 広める□failure 失敗□due to the fact that ... …という事実のために□be centered on ... …に集中する□the war →ここでは第一次世界大戦を指す

3 □concerning …に関して□confer 与える□evidence 証拠□conclusive 決定的な□there is reason to believe that ... …だと信じるに足る理由がある□stage 段階□considerable かなりの□absolute 絶対的な□outbreak（感染症の）発生

4 □despite …にもかかわらず□uncertainty 不確かさ□as to ... …に関して□micro-organism 微生物□be communicable from person to person 人から人へ伝染する□moreover そればかりか□judging from ... …から判断すると□experience 経験□probable ありそうな□whatever ... is/are …が何であれ→ここではbe動詞が省略され、「その性質が何であれ」の意□be carried about 運ばれる□be ill with ... …で具合が悪い□entirely まったく□therefore それゆえ□be regarded as ... …と見なされる□factor 要因

5 It seems probable, however, that we may expect at least local recurrences in the near future, with an increase over the normal mortality from pneumonia for perhaps several years; and certainly we should be, as far as possible, prepared to meet them by previous organization of forces and measures for attempted prevention, treatment, and scientific investigation.

6 There should be no repetition of the extensive suffering and distress which accompanied last year's pandemic. Communities should make plans now for dealing with any recurrence. The most promising way to deal with a possible recurrence is, to sum it up in a single word, 'preparedness.' And now, it is the time to prepare.

7 Evidence collected during last winter's pandemic points strongly to infected eating and drinking utensils, especially in places where food and drink are sold to the public, as being one of the modes of transmission of this disease."

---

5 □expect 予期する□local 局地的な□in the near future 近い将来に□mortality 死者数、死亡率□as far as possible できる限り□meet 対処する、立ち向かう□organization 組織化□measure(s) 対策□attempted 試みられた□prevention 予防□treatment 治療□investigation 調査

6 □repetition 繰り返し□extensive 広範囲に及ぶ□suffering 苦しみ□distress 窮状、悲嘆□accompany 付随する□community 地域社会、市区町村□deal with ... …に対処する□promising 有望な□to sum it up in a single word それを1語でまとめると→sum up は「要約する」の意□preparedness 備えておくこと、準備

7 □point strongly to ... …を強く示している□infected 汚染された□eating and drinking utensils 飲食のための器具、食器類□mode of transmission 感染経路　　　　（注／桑田）

スペイン風邪 Spanish flu (1918-1921)

第一次世界大戦中に始まり、第3波まで流行が見られた。現代と同じ予防策が100年前にも行われていたことがうかがえる。

TO-DAY'S "OUR DAY"---RALLY TO THE CALL !

Japan Times & Mail

Feb 4, 1919

1919年1月の国内感染者数は800万人、うち5万5,000人が亡くなった。

INFLUENZA DEAD 55,000 THIS YEAR

8,000,000 Epidemic Sufferers Throughout Japan Since New Year

According to sanitary officers of the Home department the total number of influenza patients in Tokyo and twenty other prefectures since January has been about 8,000,000, 55,000 of which are dead.

The Home office has sent instructions to the affected districts to take at once strict preventive measures.

OVER 100 DEATHS DAILY IN TOKYO

According to a statement by the medical department of Central Police Board the number of victims of the influenza epidemic in the city and its suburbs from January 11th to the 18th reached 706 and from the 18th to the 25th 608, showing some increase.

MINISTERS OF STATE ILL

Viscount Uchida, Foreign Minister, shows a slight improvement, his fever being reported . . . Baron Takahashi, Finance Minister, Mr. Noda, Minister of Communications, Foreign Under minister Mr. Shidehara, . . . hara, Chief of the Police Bureau, and several other officials of the Foreign office are all affected with the influenza.

The disease is also prevalent among soldiers. There are more than 350 soldiers now in the 1st garrison hospital at Miyakezaka and 15 to 20 new cases are entering the hospital every day. Among the patients are many officers including Captain Yanase of the aviation corps and Captain Kikuchi of the General staff office. Mr. Masahiko Matsukata, grand son of Marquis Matsukata, and a French flight officer, now in the Red Cross Hospital, are reported to be seriously ill.

Oct 24, 1918

東京では流行が広がり、小学校が一時閉鎖に。

INFLUENZA RAGES IN TOKYO SCHOOLS

Hundreds of Students Down With the Epidemic—Many Schools Closed

An epidemic of influenza is spreading in Tokyo, many cases being reported from all sections of the city. Many school students and pupils have been affected, and several primary schools in Fukagawa ward have been temporarily closed.

Red Cross physicians are busy examining patients and disinfecting the schools. In Onaigawa Primary School in Fukagawa, 9 teachers and over 1,000 pupils have been attacked and the school is closed.

The prefectural normal school at Aoyama has also been closed. Of the 351 students 110 have contracted the sickness. The dormitory has been closed and those in health have been sent back to their home.

Some 110 out of 264 students attending the girls normal school at Koishikawa have been also attacked by the disease, and the school has suspended the attendance of them for a week.

Cases of the temporary closing of schools owing to the increase of influenza are reported from various prefectures.

Feb 13, 1919

マスクを着用して銀座を歩く人々。

INFLUENZA MASKS ON GINZA

THE AUTHORITIES ARE TRYING TO INTRODUCE THE USE OF MASKS TO PREVENT FURTHER SPREAD OF THE EPIDEMIC.

著名人も犠牲に

スペイン風邪によって死去した人の中には、オーストリアの画家、エゴン・シーレやグスタフ・クリムト、ドイツの社会学者マックス・ウェーバーなども見られた。日本においても名をはせる人々の訃報が伝えられている。

島村抱月 (評論家・新劇指導者)

FAMOUS ACTRESS MOURNS

MISS SUMA-KO MATSUI AT MR. SHIMAMURA'S FUNERAL.

The funeral took place yesterday at Aoyama of Mr. Takitaro ("Hogetsu") Shimamura, who died on the 5th from influenza, at the age of 48.

Mr. Shimamura had achieved fame as a dramatist of the modern school, and in collaboration with Miss Suma-ko Matsui founded the new theater Geijitsu-za. Miss Matsui took the leading role in Mr. Shimamura's productions.

Mr. Shimamura had contributed much to the latter day naturalistic Japanese literature, and also translated Ibsen's "Doll's House" and other works.

Nov 08, 1918

坪内逍遥とともに「文芸協会」を設立。代表作にイプセンの『人形の家』(翻訳劇)など。写真(手前)は葬式に訪れた女優の松井須磨子。松井はこの2カ月後に後追い自殺した。

大山捨松 (日本初の女子留学生)

PRINCESS OYAMA PASSES AWAY

Marchioness Nozu Is Another Victim of Influenza Epidemic

Dowager Princess Sutematsu Oyama, widow of the late Field Marshal Prince Oyama, whose critical illness due to pneumonia caused by influenza, was reported yesterday passed away at 4.30 on Tuesday afternoon at her residence at Aoyama Onden at the age of sixty.

She was the younger sister of the late Major-General Hiroshi Yamakawa, formerly director of the Tokyo Normal School, and of Dr. Baron Yamakawa, president of the Imperial University. In 1871 she made herself famous trip to America with Miss Umeko Tsuda, Baroness Shigeko Uriu, wife of Admiral Baron Uriu, and two other ladies to study at Radcliffe and Vassar, being the pioneer Japanese women to receive advanced education in a foreign land.

Returning home in 1882 she devoted herself to the advancement of feminine education and the advancement of the social position womanhood in Japan. She took profound interest in public affairs and held the presidency of the Soldiers' Wives' Association for some time.

Princess Oyama is survived by son Lieutenant Prince Kashiwa Oyama, and three daughters. The eldest, Fuyoko, is the wife of Ichinosuke Hosokawa, son of Baron Hosokawa, the second, Tsuneko, is Countess Watanabe, widow of the late Count Watanabe the third daughter is Baroness ...

The funeral will be held at family villa at Nasuno, To prefecture, where the tomb of Field Marshal Prince Oyama, who died 1917, is situated.

NOTED SOLDIER'S WIDOW DEAD

Marchioness Tomeko Nozu, widow of the late Field Marshal Marquis Nodzu, died at her residence in Yotsuya on Tuesday morning at the age of 69, from influenza which developed into pneumonia. The funeral will take place on day morning at Aoyama cemetery.

The late Marchioness was younger sister of the late General Viscount Takashima, formerly governor-general of Formosa and later Minister of War. She is survived by a son, Major General Marquis Shinnosuke Nozu, who is the present head of the family, and four daughters. Her eldest daughter is the wife of General Uehara, Chief of General Staff, and the second is the wife of Mr. Tamio Hayashi, former managing director of the N.Y.K.

Feb 20, 1919

津田梅子らと日本初の女子留学生として渡米し、社会活動、女子教育に尽力。政治家・大山巌の妻。

Sep 27, 1918

生前の大山(右)。中央は津田梅子。旧友であるヴァッサー大学の教授の来日を歓迎。

NOTED LADY ASTRONOMER ARRIVES IN TOKYO

Dr. Caroline E. Furness, Professor of Astronomy in Vassar is on the left, in the Center is Miss Umeko Tsuda, the noted educationist and on the right the Dowager Princess Oyama (widow of the late Field Marshal Prince Oyama) both old Vassar day friends of Dr. Furness.

Dr. Caroline E. Furness, professor of Astronomy in Vassar University arrived in Tokyo yesterday. Dr. Furness reached Yokohama by the Monteagle on Monday.

Dr. Furness is visiting Japan to meet many old friends, to study the modern life and activities of Japanese womanhood and to promote good feeling between the two nations.

Many plans have been made to welcome the distinguished guest by her old friends, prominent among various functions being a reception and banquet by a joint meeting of the English Speaking Society, of which Baron Kanda is President and the Gakuyu-kai (Society of Ladies who have travelled abroad) whose president is Miss Tsuda. This will take place on Oct. 5th

from 6 p.m. at the Fujimi-ken in Fujimi-cho, Kudansaka-ue. About 150 members and friends are expected to attend, among them, besides the guest of honor and officers of the society, Dowager Princess Oyama, Viscount Kaneko, Baroness Uryu, Baroness Megata, Dr. Nitobe, and Dr. Asakawa of Yale. Several of these ladies and gentlemen will deliver addresses of welcome.

SARS (2002-03)／MERS (2012)

2000年初めには中国を中心にSARS(重症急性呼吸器症候群)が流行、その10年後にはアラブ首長国連邦、カタール、ヨルダンといった中東地域を中心にMERS(中東呼吸器症候群)の感染が見られた。どちらもコロナウイルス(CoV)の一種。

THE JAPAN TIMES • SATURDAY, MAY 3, 2003　13

BEST OF . . .

The Observer
THE AWARD-WINNING NEWSPAPER

BECKHAMS PLAN NEW REIGN IN SPAIN
With soccer star David Beckham and his pop star wife Victoria — better known as Posh Spice — apparently close to sealing a move to Madrid, what can Britain's 'First Couple' expect from Spain's capital? **Page 15**

Threat posed by SARS worsens
Death rate double WHO's estimate, but battle is being won

By GABY HINSLIFF,
NICOLA BYRNE
and JOHN AGLIONBY

SARS deals tourism in China a telling blow

By TOM TEMPLETON

May 03, 2003

SARSの致死率は約10%(当時)。観光業への打撃も報じられた。

IN BRIEF

MERS outbreak feared at Saudi hajj

Geneva AFP-JIJI
Virologists are casting a worried eye on this year's Islamic hajj pilgrimage to Saudi Arabia as they struggle with the enigmatic, deadly virus known as MERS, which is striking hardest in the kingdom.

Little is known about the pathogen that causes Middle East respiratory syndrome beyond the fact that it can be lethal by causing respiratory problems, pneumonia and kidney failure. It can be transmitted between humans, but unlike its cousin the SARS virus, which sparked a scare a decade ago, it does not seem very contagious.

Even so, the mass gathering of the hajj provides a perfect opportunity for any respiratory virus to spread at the two holiest Muslim shrines in Mecca and Medina, and then travel around the globe as pilgrims return home.

This year's event will occur in October as the Northern Hemisphere slides into the season for coughs and sneezes.

Experts point first and foremost to figuring out the basics of the MERS coronavirus and how it is transmitted.

Forty MERS patients have died, an extremely high rate of 52 percent. But the tally of people who have fallen ill with MERS but not been diagnosed with it, or who may have been infected but not developed symptoms, is unknown.

Jul 02, 2013

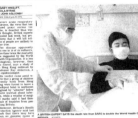

専門家はサウジアラビアのメッカ、メディナへの巡礼によるウイルス感染拡大を懸念。

Aug 10, 2013

ヒトコブラクダから抗体が検出され、感染源である可能性が浮かび上がった。

Deadly transport? A camel walks past a water spring near the shores of the Dead Sea in Jordan. AFP-JIJI

Camels may be behind spread of mysterious MERS

London
AP

Scientists have found an intriguing clue that suggests camels might somehow be involved in infecting people in the Middle East with the mysterious MERS virus.

Since the virus was first identified last September, there have been 94 illnesses, including 46 deaths, from Middle East respiratory syndrome, mostly in Saudi Arabia. Aside from several clusters where the virus has likely spread between people, experts have largely been stumped as to how patients got infected.

In a preliminary study published Friday, European scientists found traces of antibodies against the MERS virus in dromedary (one-humped) camels but not the virus itself. Finding antibodies means the camels were at one point infected with MERS or a similar virus before fighting off the infection.

The antibodies were found in all 50 camel blood samples from Oman, compared with 15 of 105 samples from Spanish camels. Animals from the Netherlands and Chile were tested for comparison with those from Oman. No MERS antibodies were found in tests done on cows, sheep or goats.

"Finding the (MERS) virus is like finding a needle in a haystack, but finding the antibodies at least gives you an indication of where to look," said Marion Koopmans, chief of virology at the Netherlands National Institute for Public Health and the Environment, the study's senior author. "What this tells us is that there's something circulating in camels that looks related to MERS."

The study was published in the Lancet Infectious Diseases. Koopmans expects results will be similar for other camel populations across the Middle East.

MERS is part of a family of coronaviruses that can cause the common cold as well as SARS, which sparked a global outbreak in 2003.

Saudi Arabia health officials, in a letter this week to the New England Journal of Medicine, documented seven new infections of MERS in health workers, including some mild cases.

MERS is now closely related to another strain found in bats that migrate to and from the six natural source. Some experts think bats might be infecting other animals like camels with MERS before passing it to humans. MERS can cause symptoms including fever, cough, breathing problems, pneumonia and kidney failure. There is no known treatment or cure.

その他の社会問題

1月13日、使用済みMOXが取り出される四国電力伊方原発3号機

Broaden the fight against demographic woes

人口統計学的な難局との闘いを広げよ

January 9, 2020　　　　　　　　　●Tracks 41-45 / 訳 pp. 110-112

Track 41

1　If the number of newborns each year is an indicator of the hope that young adults have in the nation's future—so that they feel secure enough to have a family—Japan's prospects are fairly grim. The estimated number of babies born in this country in 2019 fell more than 50,000 from the previous year to 864,000, the lowest in the past 120 years. That is roughly 40 percent of the figure in the mid-1970s, when the nation's total fertility rate—the average number of children a woman gives birth to in her lifetime—was last at the level required to sustain the population.

2　As the elderly account for a larger proportion of the population, the number of deaths last year is estimated to have reached a postwar high of 1.37 million. The natural decline of the population—the number of deaths minus that of births—hit another high of 512,000. Japan lost a population equivalent to that of Tottori Prefecture (550,000) in a single year. The bad news is that the aging and shrinking of the nation's population is forecast to accelerate in the decades to come.

日本の人口の高齢化と減少の問題が指摘されて久しいが、根本的な解決ばかりか、有効な対策すらも見えていないのが現状だ。若者たちが安心して子育てできる社会を作るためには、政府の政策任せにするのではなく、社会一丸となった取り組みが必要である。

1
- ☐ [タイトル] broaden 広げる
- ☐ [タイトル] demographic 人口統計学的な
- ☐ [タイトル] woe 難局
- ☐ newborn 新生児
- ☐ indicator 指標
- ☐ secure 安心した
- ☐ prospect 見通し
- ☐ fairly かなり
- ☐ grim 厳しい
- ☐ estimated number 推計数
- ☐ previous 前の
- ☐ roughly およそ
- ☐ mid-1970s 1970年代半ば→mid-は「真ん中の」の意
- ☐ total fertility rate 合計特殊出生率
- ☐ give birth to ... …を出産する
- ☐ lifetime 生涯、一生
- ☐ be required to do ～するのに必要とされる
- ☐ sustain 維持する
- ☐ population 人口

2
- ☐ the elderly 高齢者
- ☐ account for ... …を占める
- ☐ proportion 割合
- ☐ be estimated to do ～すると推計される
- ☐ postwar high 戦後の最高記録→このhighは名詞
- ☐ natural decline 自然減
- ☐ equivalent to ... …に等しい、相当する
- ☐ prefecture 県
- ☐ aging 高齢化
- ☐ shrinking 縮小
- ☐ be forecast to do ～すると予測される
- ☐ accelerate 加速する
- ☐ in the decades to come これからやってくる数十年間で

Track 42

3 The problem of rapid aging and decline of Japan's population with a falling number of births is nothing new. Since the 1990s, the government has taken steps to support young couples in child rearing, such as increasing the capacity of day care services. In October, it began offering free day care services and preschool education for children 3 to 5 years old. However, these efforts have failed to produce tangible effects in reversing the long-term trend of declining births. Instead, the data show that our population is aging and shrinking more rapidly than previously forecast.

4 The government's efforts remain insufficient. Japan spends 1.3 percent of its GDP on family-related public expenses such as nursery services and child allowances—roughly one-third of the level in European states that maintain higher fertility rates. But the experience of the past decades also indicates that government policies alone cannot reverse the trend.

Track 43

5 Along with scrutinizing the shortcomings of government policies, more broad-based efforts are needed to address the demographic woes, ranging from reviewing the social mechanism in which the burden of child-raising and household chores tends to focus on women, to fixing the prevalent labor practices at Japanese companies, such as the chronically long working hours that prevent both fathers and mothers from spending time with their families.

3
- ☐ rapid 急速な
- ☐ falling 減っている
- ☐ be nothing new 新しいことではない、今に始まったことではない
- ☐ take steps 措置を講じる
- ☐ child rearing 子育て
- ☐ capacity 収容能力、定員
- ☐ day care service 保育サービス
  → day care には「高齢者介護」の意味もある
- ☐ preschool education 幼児教育
  → preschool は「就学前の」の意

- ☐ fail to *do* ～することができない
- ☐ tangible 目に見える、具体的な
- ☐ effect 効果
- ☐ reverse 反転させる
- ☐ long-term 長期的な
- ☐ trend 傾向
- ☐ instead それどころか
- ☐ age 高齢化する
- ☐ shrink 縮小する
- ☐ previously 以前に

4
- ☐ remain …のままである
- ☐ insufficient 不十分な
- ☐ GDP 国内総生産→gross domestic product
- ☐ family-related 家族関連の
- ☐ public expenses 公費
- ☐ nursery 保育園

- ☐ child allowance 児童手当
- ☐ one-third 3分の1
- ☐ maintain 維持する
- ☐ experience 経験
- ☐ indicate 示す
- ☐ policy 政策

5
- ☐ scrutinize 精査する
- ☐ shortcoming 欠点
- ☐ broad-based 広範囲に及ぶ
- ☐ address 対処する
- ☐ range from A to B AからBにまで及ぶ
- ☐ review 見直す
- ☐ mechanism 仕組み
- ☐ burden 負担
- ☐ child-raising 子育て

- ☐ household chore 家事
- ☐ tend to *do* ～する傾向がある
- ☐ focus on ... …に集中する
- ☐ fix 修正する
- ☐ prevalent 広く行き渡っている
- ☐ practice 慣行
- ☐ chronically 慢性的に
- ☐ prevent ... from *doing* …が～することを妨げる

6 While the choice of having children is up to each individual, we need to at least secure a social and economic environment where young people are not deterred by financial insecurity from having children—as is believed to have been the case with many of the "employment ice age" generation who graduated from school after the early 1990s collapse of the bubble boom.

Track 44

7 The falling population of children—which will translate into a shrinking pool of workers in the coming decades—endangers the future growth of the nation's economy by eroding its capacity to generate wealth and capping the base for consumer spending. The decline in the working age population (which fell from 87.16 million in 1995 to 75.45 million in 2018 and is forecast to decline to 68.75 million in 2030 and 59.78 million in 2040) shakes the foundation of the social security programs, in which premiums paid by the working generations cover the benefits for the growing elderly ranks.

6
- □ choice 選択
- □ be up to ... …次第である
- □ individual 個人
- □ secure 確保する、守る
- □ environment 環境
- □ be deterred from *doing* 〜すること を思いとどまらせられる
- □ financial 金銭的な
- □ insecurity 不安
- □ as is the case with ... …に当てはま るように
- □ employment ice age 就職氷河期
- □ generation 世代
- □ graduate from ... …を卒業する
- □ collapse 崩壊
- □ bubble boom バブル景気

7
- □ translate into ... 結果として…につな がる
- □ pool 要員
- □ coming 来るべき
- □ endanger 危険にさらす
- □ erode 損なう
- □ generate 生成する、生み出す
- □ wealth 富
- □ cap 上限を定める
- □ consumer spending 個人消費
- □ working age population 生産年齢 人口→日本では15歳から64歳までの 人口を指す
- □ shake the foundation 根幹を揺るがす
- □ social security program 社会保障 制度
- □ premium 保険料
- □ benefit(s) 給付金
- □ rank （社会的な）階層

8   The aging and shrinking population makes it harder to keep up the various systems that have so far sustained this country. A complicating factor is the population flight to Tokyo, which has the lowest fertility rate among the nation's 47 prefectures. Despite the government's pledge to reverse the trend under the "regional revitalization" slogan, the net population inflow into the greater Tokyo area remains unabated. The very survival of many municipalities will be in doubt in the not-so-distant future. In these areas, maintaining administrative services for residents under the current framework of local government is going to become difficult, while many small municipalities in rural depopulated regions are finding it increasingly hard to maintain their assemblies—the very foundation of local autonomy.

Track 45

9   The nation's current demographic woes are the outcome of a long-term trend since the 1970s, and the further aging and shrinking of the population is deemed unavoidable—since the number of women in primary child-bearing age has already declined significantly. There were 13 million women aged 25 to 39 in 2000; today, they number 9.7 million. The total fertility rate remains near its historic low, and a modest recovery in the rate is not expected to reverse the decline in the number of newborns and the falling population in coming decades.

8
- □ keep up ... …を持続させる
- □ various さまざまな
- □ so far これまで
- □ complicating 複雑にしている
- □ factor 要因
- □ population flight to ... …への人口流出→このflightは「脱出」の意
- □ despite …にもかかわらず
- □ pledge 公約
- □ regional revitalization 地域の再活性化、地方創生
- □ net 正味の
- □ inflow 流入
- □ the greater Tokyo area 首都圏
- □ unabated 衰えない
- □ municipality 市区町村
- □ be in doubt 疑わしい、不確かで
- □ in the not-so-distant future それほど遠くない将来に
- □ administrative 行政の
- □ resident 住民
- □ current 現行の
- □ framework 枠組み
- □ local government 地方自治体
- □ rural 地方の
- □ depopulated 過疎の
- □ increasingly ますます
- □ assembly 議会
- □ autonomy 自治

9
- □ outcome 結果
- □ further 一層の
- □ be deemed ... …であると思われる
- □ unavoidable 避けられない
- □ primary 主要な、中心的な
- □ child-bearing age 出産適齢期
- □ significantly 著しく
- □ number …の数になる→このnumberは動詞
- □ modest ささやかな
- □ recovery 回復
- □ be expected to *do* ～すると期待される

10   There are no quick remedies for the rapid aging and shrinking of Japan's population, but inaction will only make matters worse. We need to explore and identify effective measures, and steadily implement them. Equally important will be to adjust the nation's various systems and policies to the demographic reality before it's too late. With the aging of the population, annual social security expenses such as pension, medical services and nursing care for the elderly are forecast to hit ¥140 trillion in 2025, and balloon to ¥190 trillion in 2040—when the aging of the population is forecast to near its peak. Introducing necessary reforms and adjustments to these systems will contribute to easing the younger generation's sense of insecurity for the nation's future.

10
- □ quick remedy 即効薬
- □ inaction 不作為、何もしないこと
- □ make matters worse 事態を悪化させる
- □ explore 模索する
- □ identify 特定する
- □ effective 効果的な
- □ measure(s) 対策
- □ steadily 着実に
- □ implement 実行する
- □ adjust 調整する、手直しする

- □ annual 年間の
- □ pension 年金
- □ medical 医療の
- □ nursing care 看護、介護
- □ trillion 1兆
- □ balloon to ... …に膨れ上がる
- □ introduce 導入する
- □ reform 改革
- □ adjustment 手直し、調整
- □ contribute to ... …に貢献する
- □ ease 和らげる

Coming to terms with what's behind the Sagamihara killings

相模原障害者施設殺傷事件の背後にある問題

February 13, 2020　　　　　●Tracks 46-49 / 訳 pp. 113-114

Track 46

1　The ongoing trial of Satoshi Uematsu, accused of killing 19 people and injuring many others at a care home for people with mental disabilities in Sagamihara, Kanagawa Prefecture, in July 2016, should provide an opportunity for all of us to reflect on whether he is alone in judging the value of other people's lives on the basis of how useful or productive they are to society.

2　Until just a quarter century ago, this country had a law that authorized the forced sterilization of people with mental disabilities in order to prevent the birth of "eugenically inferior" offspring, and it was only last year that a compensation program was legislated for the victims and they were offered a government apology. Discrimination against people with disabilities remains deeply rooted in our society. Instead of only highlighting the accused's distorted—and despicable—views toward his victims, we should think hard about whether society at large shares any of his ideas behind the grisly murders.

Track 47

3　Since surrendering himself to police after the fatal knife rampage against the care home residents four years ago, Uematsu, a former employee of the facility, has insisted that he killed the victims to do good for society as people with heavy disabilities are useless and only bring misfortune, and thus should be euthanized. He has reiterated similar arguments in the trial that opened last month. He claims he is mentally competent to stand trial, rebuffing the plea of innocence on grounds of insanity made by his own lawyers.

2016年に相模原市の知的障害者福祉施設で元職員が多くの利用者を殺傷した事件は、その残忍さとともに犯人が知的障害者に対して一貫して抱き続けた思想によっても世間に戦慄を走らせた。犯人は2020年3月に横浜地裁での裁判員裁判で死刑判決を受け、自らの控訴取り下げによって死刑が確定している。

1
- ☐ [タイトル]come to terms with ... …を受け入れる
- ☐ ongoing 現在進行中の
- ☐ (be) accused of *doing* 〜したという罪に問われている
- ☐ care home 介護福祉施設
- ☐ mental disability 知的障害
- ☐ opportunity 機会
- ☐ reflect on ... …を振り返ってよく考える、自省する
- ☐ on the basis of ... …を基準にして、…に基づいて
- ☐ productive 生産的な→「労働生産性が高い」から「子どもが産める」という非常に差別的な意味まで広く含まれる

2
- ☐ authorize 認可する
- ☐ forced 強制的な
- ☐ sterilization 不妊手術
- ☐ eugenically 優生学的に
- ☐ inferior 劣っている
- ☐ offspring 子孫
- ☐ it is only A that ... A になってやっと…となる
- ☐ compensation 補償
- ☐ legislate 法制化する
- ☐ apology 謝罪
- ☐ discrimination 差別
- ☐ deeply rooted in ... …に根深く存在する
- ☐ highlight …に焦点を当てる、…ばかりを取り上げる
- ☐ the accused 被告人
- ☐ distorted ゆがんだ
- ☐ despicable 卑劣な
- ☐ at large 一般の、全体の→名詞のあとに付ける
- ☐ grisly おぞましい

3
- ☐ surrender *oneself* to police 自首する、出頭する
- ☐ fatal 死亡者の出た
- ☐ rampage 凶行、暴力事件
- ☐ facility 施設
- ☐ do good for ... …のためになることをする
- ☐ misfortune 不幸
- ☐ euthanize 安楽死させる
- ☐ reiterate 繰り返して言う
- ☐ argument 主張
- ☐ mentally competent （精神的に）責任能力がある
- ☐ stand trial 裁判を受ける
- ☐ rebuff 退ける、拒絶する
- ☐ make a plea 申し立てる
- ☐ innocence 無罪
- ☐ on grounds of ... …を根拠とした
- ☐ insanity 精神異常

4   It would be easy to dismiss his words as the twisted view of a mass murderer trying to justify his crime. But a large number of messages posted online since the murders have reportedly expressed support for his views—an indication that popular prejudice and discrimination against people with disabilities linger on. The lay judge trial at the Yokohama District Court, which is scheduled to hand down its ruling in mid-March, needs to explore how Uematsu came to embrace his distorted way of thinking. And we must ponder what can be done for society as a whole to reject such a view.

`Track 48`

5   It was only in 1996 that the Eugenic Protection Law—which authorized the sterilization of people with intellectual disabilities, mental illnesses and hereditary diseases, even without the consent of the people undergoing the operations—was abolished. In the nearly half century since the law was enacted in 1948, operations were performed on a total of some 25,000 people—at least 16,500 of them against their will. But it then took more than 20 years for the state to provide relief and an apology for the victims, who were deprived by government policy of their right to have children.

6   Even today, there remains a way of thinking that judges people and their value on the basis of whether they are productive and useful to society. People supporting victims of the Eugenic Protection Law as well as former Hansen's disease patients, who were subjected to forced segregation for decades without medical grounds, say they are the victims of a misguided government policy that sought to exclude people whose presence was inconvenient to society. Behind the murders at the Sagamihara care home, they charge, is the eugenics beliefs that the government spread through its policies and failed to eradicate even after relevant laws were scrapped.

4
- □ dismiss A as B　AをBとして片付ける
- □ twisted　ゆがんだ
- □ mass murderer　大量殺害者→massは「大人数、多数」の意
- □ justify　正当化する
- □ post　投稿する
- □ reportedly　報道によると
- □ support for ...　…に対する支持
- □ indication　表れ
- □ popular　一般に広まっている
- □ prejudice　偏見

- □ linger on　根強く残る
- □ lay judge trial　裁判員裁判→layは「素人の」の意
- □ hand down　（判決を）言い渡す
- □ ruling　判決
- □ explore　深く探る
- □ embrace　（考えを）抱く
- □ ponder　じっくり考える
- □ ... as a whole　…全体で
- □ reject　退ける

5
- □ the Eugenic Protection Law　優生保護法
- □ intellectual　知的な
- □ hereditary　遺伝性の
- □ consent　同意
- □ undergo　（手術などを）受ける
- □ abolish　廃止する
- □ enact　法制化［制定］する

- □ perform an operation on ...　…に手術を施す
- □ some　（数字の前で）約…
- □ against *one's* will　～の意思に反して、強制的に
- □ state　国
- □ relief　救済措置
- □ deprive A of B　AからBを奪う

6
- □ there remains ...　…がまだ残っている
- □ Hansen's disease　ハンセン病→以前の呼称は「らい病」
- □ be subjected to ...　…を受ける
- □ segregation　隔離
- □ ground(s)　根拠
- □ misguided　（判断を）誤った
- □ seek to *do*　～しようと努める→soughtはseekの過去形・過去分詞形
- □ exclude　排除する

- □ presence　存在
- □ inconvenient　不都合な
- □ charge　非難する
- □ eugenics　優生学
- □ spread　広める→過去形・過去分詞形もspread
- □ eradicate　根絶する
- □ relevant　関連する
- □ scrap　廃止する

Track 49

7   Just before the murders took place in 2016, legislation was enacted that prohibited discrimination by government offices and private businesses against people with disabilities. In a Cabinet Office survey taken the following year, however, more than 80 percent of the respondents said they believe that such discrimination and prejudice persist in society. Plans to build care facilities for people with intellectual/mental disabilities often face opposition from neighboring residents, with some of them eventually being canceled as a result. The fact that most of the victims of the 2016 murders at the Sagamihara care home are being kept anonymous in the trial is yet another reminder of the distorted views that all too many people hold toward the disabled and their families.

8   To help prevent a recurrence of abhorrent crimes against people with disabilities, society as a whole needs to come to grips with the widespread prejudice and discrimination against such people, and take steps to amend the situation.

7
- ☐ legislation 法律
- ☐ prohibit 禁止する
- ☐ government office 行政機関 → local governmentと呼ばれる地方自治体なども含む
- ☐ private business 民間企業
- ☐ Cabinet Office 内閣府
- ☐ take a survey 調査をする
- ☐ respondent 回答者
- ☐ persist 根強く残る
- ☐ face opposition from ... …からの反対に遭う
- ☐ eventually 最終的に
- ☐ cancel （計画を）中止にする
- ☐ anonymous 匿名の
- ☐ yet another またもう一つの
- ☐ reminder of ... …を思い出させるもの
- ☐ hold a view 考えを抱く
- ☐ all too many ... あまりにも多くの… →数の多さを嘆く表現
- ☐ the disabled 障害者

8
- ☐ recurrence 再発
- ☐ abhorrent 忌まわしい
- ☐ come to grips with ... …を把握しようとする、…に（目をそらさず）正面から向き合う
- ☐ widespread 広まっている
- ☐ take steps 方策を取る
- ☐ amend 改善する、改める

Review the nation's quest for a nuclear fuel cycle

見直すべき核燃料サイクルの探求

February 20, 2020

●Tracks 50-53 / 訳 pp. 115-116

Track 50

1 The uncertain fate of the spent mixed-oxide (MOX) fuel removed from two nuclear power reactors in western Japan last month—for the first time since the commercial use of plutonium-uranium fuel in light water reactors began about a decade ago—is yet another sign of the stalemate over the government's nuclear fuel cycle policy. While the government maintains that all spent nuclear fuel will be reprocessed for reuse as fuel for nuclear reactors, there are no facilities in this country that can reprocess spent MOX fuel so it will remain indefinitely in storage pools at the nuclear plants.

2 A reprocessing plant owned by Japan Nuclear Fuel Ltd. that is under construction in Rokkasho, Aomori Prefecture, can only handle spent uranium fuel. No concrete plans have been made for building a second plant capable of reprocessing spent MOX fuel. Completion of the Rokkasho plant itself has been delayed for years amid an endless series of technical glitches resulting in huge cost overruns since construction began in the early 1990s. When the plant is completed and begins operating it will likely only add to Japan's plutonium stockpile. This is because the use of plutonium in MOX fuel remains sluggish due to the slow restart of reactors idled following the 2011 meltdowns at the Fukushima No. 1 nuclear power plant operated by Tokyo Electric Power Company Holdings Inc.

再利用をうたいながらも、そのめどが立たないまま使用済み核燃料の備蓄が増えていく現状は放置できない。脱原発の動きの一方、気候変動対策として化石燃料の使用削減の流れもある。エネルギー政策全般を見据えたさまざまな観点からの見直しが必要であろう。

1
- □ [タイトル]quest 探求
- □ [タイトル]nuclear fuel cycle 核燃料サイクル
- □ uncertain 不確かな
- □ spent 使用済みの
- □ mixed-oxide fuel 混合酸化物燃料→再処理で取り出したプルトニウムを、ウランと混ぜ合わせた燃料
- □ remove 取り出す
- □ nuclear power reactor 原子炉
- □ commercial 商業的な
- □ plutonium-uranium fuel プルトニウム・ウラン燃料→MOX燃料のこと
- □ light water reactor 軽水炉
- □ yet another さらにもう一つの
- □ stalemate 行き詰まり
- □ maintain 主張する
- □ reprocess 再処理する
- □ reuse 再利用
- □ facility 施設
- □ indefinitely 無期限に
- □ storage pool 貯蔵プール

2
- □ reprocessing plant 再処理工場
- □ Japan Nuclear Fuel Ltd. 日本原燃株式会社→Ltd.はLimitedの略
- □ be under construction 建設中である
- □ prefecture 県
- □ concrete 具体的な
- □ capable of *doing* ～する能力がある
- □ completion 完成
- □ delay 遅らせる
- □ amid …のさなかに
- □ glitch 小さな問題、不具合
- □ result in ... …の結果になる
- □ overrun 超過
- □ complete 完成させる
- □ operate 操業する
- □ likely おそらく
- □ add to ... …を増やす
- □ stockpile 備蓄
- □ sluggish 低調な
- □ due to ... …のために
- □ restart 再稼働、再スタート
- □ idle （運転を）停止する
- □ meltdown 炉心融解
- □ Tokyo Electric Power Company Holdings Inc. 東京電力ホールディングス株式会社→Inc.はIncorporatedの略

Track 51

3　Instead of shelving hard decisions on the nuclear fuel cycle policy any further, the government and the power industry need to candidly assess the prospects of the policy and proceed with a long-overdue review.

4　Under the policy that touts efficient use of uranium resources, fuel assemblies spent at nuclear power plants will be removed from the reactors to extract plutonium, which will be blended with uranium to make the MOX fuel. What were removed from the reactors at Shikoku Electric Power Co.'s Ikata plant in Ehime Prefecture and Kansai Electric Power Co.'s Takahama plant in Fukui Prefecture in January are the MOX fuel rods that were installed in 2010. The government maintains that it's technologically feasible to reprocess spent MOX fuel, but experts are doubtful about the efficiency of this practice.

Track 52

5　Initially, the policy assumed a transition to fast-breeder reactors in Japan's nuclear power generation. Touted to produce more plutonium than it consumes as fuel, a fast-breeder reactor was deemed a dream technology in this resource-scarce country. However, Monju, the nation's sole prototype fast-breeder reactor— on which more than ¥1 trillion was spent—was decommissioned in 2016 after sitting idle for much of the time since it first went online in 1994 due to a series of accidents and troubles. The government sought to continue research on next-generation fast reactors in a joint project with France, but that bid has been in limbo since Paris decided to substantially scale back the project in light of the abundance of uranium resources, which cast doubts over its economic feasibility.

3
- □ shelve 先送りにする、棚上げにする
- □ any further これ以上
- □ power industry 電力業界
- □ candidly 公正に
- □ assess 評価する
- □ prospect 見通し
- □ proceed with ... …を進める
- □ long-overdue 延び延びになっている →もっと早くしておくべきだったという含みがある

4
- □ tout ほめる、宣伝する
- □ efficient 効果的な
- □ resources 資源
- □ fuel assembly 燃料集合体→数十本の燃料棒（fuel rod）を束ねたもの
- □ extract 抽出する
- □ be blended with ... …と混ぜられる
- □ Shikoku Electric Power Co. 四国電力株式会社→Co. は Company の略
- □ Kansai Electric Power Co. 関西電力株式会社
- □ fuel rod 燃料棒
- □ install 装荷する→原子炉に燃料を入れること
- □ technologically （科学）技術的に
- □ feasible 実現可能な
- □ expert 専門家
- □ doubtful 疑いを抱いて
- □ efficiency 効率
- □ practice （仕事などの）やり方

5
- □ initially 当初は
- □ assume 想定する
- □ transition 移行
- □ fast-breeder reactor 高速増殖炉
- □ power generation 発電
- □ consume 消費する
- □ be deemed …であると思われる
- □ resource-scarce 資源の乏しい
- □ prototype 原型
- □ trillion 1兆
- □ decommission 廃炉にする
- □ sit idle 運転を停止した状態である→このsitは「…のままである」の意
- □ go online 稼働する
- □ seek to *do* ～しようと努める→sought はseekの過去形・過去分詞形
- □ continue 継続する
- □ next-generation 次世代の
- □ bid 努力、取り組み
- □ be in limbo 中ぶらりんである
- □ substantially 大幅に
- □ scale back ... …を縮小する
- □ in light of ... …を考慮して
- □ abundance 豊富さ
- □ cast doubts over ... …に疑問を投げ掛ける
- □ economic feasibility 経済的可能性→採算などの経済的な観点からの可能性のこと

6 As completion of the reprocessing plant in Rokkasho continues to be pushed back, some 15,000 tons of spent nuclear fuel is stored at nuclear power plants across Japan. Combined with 3,000 tons kept in the storage pool at the Rokkasho plant, the total comes to around 18,000 tons. The volume will only increase if more reactors are restarted without the launch of the reprocessing plant, and the capacity of storage pools at power plants is limited.

Track 53

7 On the other hand, Japan is under pressure to utilize its 45-ton stockpile of plutonium as fuel due to proliferation concerns. As the Monju project went nowhere, the government and the power industry have pursued the use of MOX fuel in conventional light water reactors since around 2010. However, the use of MOX fuels has remained slow following the shuttering of most of the nation's nuclear plants after the 2011 Fukushima disaster. Currently, MOX fuel is used in only four reactors across the country—far below the 16 to 18 planned prior to the Fukushima accident. There are also doubts about the economic viability of the use of MOX fuel, which is more costly than conventional nuclear fuel.

8 It seems clear that the nuclear fuel cycle policy is stuck in a stalemate, but neither the government nor the power industry will accept that—apparently because abandoning the program would seriously impact the nuclear energy policy. An alternative to reprocessing is to bury the spent fuel deep underground—a method reportedly adopted in some countries. But then the spent fuel—which has so far been stored as a resource to be processed for reuse—will be turned into nuclear waste, raising the politically sensitive question of where to dispose of it. That, however, is a question that cannot be averted given Japan's use of nuclear power. It should not be used as an excuse for maintaining the quest for the elusive nuclear fuel cycle. It's time to review the policy.

6
- [ ] push back ... …を先延ばしにする
- [ ] store 保管する
- [ ] across Japan 日本各地で
- [ ] combined with ... …と合わせて
- [ ] the total comes to ... 合計は…に達する
- [ ] around 約…
- [ ] volume 量
- [ ] launch 開始
- [ ] capacity 容量

7
- [ ] on the other hand その一方で
- [ ] be under pressure to *do* 〜する必要に迫られている
- [ ] utilize 活用する
- [ ] proliferation 拡散→ここでは核兵器の拡散を指す
- [ ] concern 懸念
- [ ] go nowhere 行き詰まる
- [ ] pursue 追求する
- [ ] conventional 従来型の
- [ ] following …後に、…を受けて
- [ ] shuttering 停止
- [ ] disaster 大惨事
- [ ] currently 現在
- [ ] across the country 全国で
- [ ] far below …よりはるかに少ない
- [ ] prior to ... …以前の
- [ ] viability 実現可能性
- [ ] costly 費用がかかる

8
- [ ] be stuck in ... （よくない状況に）はまっている
- [ ] accept 認める
- [ ] apparently どうやら…らしい
- [ ] abandon 放棄する
- [ ] seriously 深刻に
- [ ] impact 影響を及ぼす
- [ ] alternative 代案
- [ ] deep underground 地中深くに
- [ ] method 方法
- [ ] reportedly 伝えられるところでは
- [ ] adopt 採用する
- [ ] but then とはいえ
- [ ] process 処理する
- [ ] be turned into ... …と化す
- [ ] nuclear waste 核廃棄物
- [ ] politically 政治的に
- [ ] sensitive 慎重な対応を要する
- [ ] dispose of ... …を処理する
- [ ] avert 避ける
- [ ] given …を考慮すると→このgivenは前置詞
- [ ] excuse 口実、言い訳
- [ ] elusive 達成し難い
- [ ] it's time to *do* 今こそ〜すべき時である

Online abuse is a silent pandemic affecting millions

ネット上の中傷は多くを苦しめる静かなパンデミック

June 11, 2020

●Tracks 54-60 / 訳 pp. 117-119

Track 54

1 News that Hana Kimura, a 22-year-old pro wrestler who starred in the popular reality show "Terrace House," apparently committed suicide after receiving hundreds of hate messages sent shock waves across the nation late last month. It was a tragic reminder that the government has been slow in taking measures to protect victims of cyberbullying.

2 "Some people say that you should just refrain from reading these comments online. But social media has become an essential part of our lives and it is extremely difficult not to see them," Shiori Ito, a journalist and symbol of Japan's #MeToo movement, stated at a recent news conference.

Track 55

3 Ms. Ito has been receiving online hate messages for more than three years after going public with a rape accusation against Noriyuki Yamaguchi, a former Washington bureau chief of Tokyo Broadcasting System Television Inc. Some of the hate messages were directed at her family and friends as well. After scrutinizing some 700,000 messages online, she filed a lawsuit on Monday against cartoonist Toshiko Hasumi and two others for defaming her on Twitter. Ms. Ito claims Ms. Hasumi's cartoon defamed her by suggesting she filed a false rape accusation and is pretending to be a rape victim.

匿名であるのをいいことに、ネット上での個人への度を越した誹謗中傷がますます増えており、その攻撃対象は有名人に限らない。被害者保護のための法整備はもちろん、各自がSNSの使い方をあらためて考え、投稿や拡散の前にその内容を見直すことも大切であろう。

1
- ☐ [タイトル]abuse 虐待、中傷
- ☐ [タイトル]pandemic パンデミック（感染症の世界的大流行）
- ☐ [タイトル]affect 影響を与える
- ☐ star 主演する
- ☐ reality show リアリティー番組
- ☐ apparently どうやら…らしい
- ☐ commit suicide 自殺する
- ☐ hate message 嫌がらせのメッセージ
- ☐ send shock waves 衝撃を与える
- ☐ reminder 思い出させるもの
- ☐ take measures 対策を取る
- ☐ victim 犠牲者
- ☐ cyberbullying ネットいじめ

2
- ☐ refrain from *doing* ～することを控える
- ☐ social media ソーシャルメディア
- ☐ essential 重要な、欠かせない
- ☐ extremely 極めて
- ☐ #MeToo movement 「#MeToo」運動→セクハラなどの被害を告発する運動。#MeTooは「私も」を意味するme tooにハッシュタグ（#）を付けたもの
- ☐ state 述べる
- ☐ news conference 記者会見

3
- ☐ go public with ... …を公表する
- ☐ rape 性的暴行
- ☐ accusation 告発
- ☐ bureau 支局
- ☐ Tokyo Broadcasting System Television Inc. 株式会社TBSテレビ →Inc.はIncorporatedの略
- ☐ be directed at ... …に向けられる
- ☐ scrutinize 丹念に調べる
- ☐ file a lawsuit against ... …に対して訴訟を起こす
- ☐ cartoonist 漫画家
- ☐ defame 名誉を傷付ける
- ☐ cartoon 漫画
- ☐ false 虚偽の
- ☐ pretend to be ... …であると装う

4 As more and more people use social media today, cyberbullying is emerging as a potentially life-threatening concern. It's time for the government and social networking services to hammer out effective measures to prevent online abuse.

5 One of the main reasons why such abuse is ubiquitous is that people can make defamatory posts anonymously and it is almost impossible to detect them because of the complex procedures involved.

6 To identify such individuals in Japan, victims have to go through multiple court proceedings. First, they must ask the court for a temporary injunction to request social networking service operators, such as Twitter, to disclose the IP addresses of individuals who posted defamatory messages. By identifying the IP addresses, victims can find out which internet service providers have been used to post the messages.

7 Second, they must file a lawsuit to request that the internet service provider disclose personal information, such as names and addresses. Only after going through this procedure, victims can file lawsuits against the offenders.

8 Successfully taking each step remains difficult as well. For instance, even if a victim manages to obtain the IP address of the poster, they must prove their rights were infringed upon by the spread of the post in order to obtain personal information from the internet service provider. If the post was made from a device that is used by multiple people, for example a PC at an internet cafe, it is almost impossible to identify who made the post.

4
- ☐ emerge as ... …として現れる
- ☐ potentially 潜在的に、…かもしれない
- ☐ life-threatening 命に関わる
- ☐ concern 関心事、懸念事項
- ☐ social networking service ソーシャル・ネットワーキング・サービス、SNS
- ☐ hammer out ... …を打ち出す
- ☐ effective 効果的な

5
- ☐ ubiquitous 至るところにある
- ☐ defamatory 中傷的な
- ☐ post 投稿
- ☐ anonymously 匿名で
- ☐ detect 見つける
- ☐ complex 複雑な
- ☐ procedure 手順

6
- ☐ identify （身元を）特定する
- ☐ individual 個人
- ☐ go through ... …を経る
- ☐ multiple 複数の
- ☐ court proceedings 訴訟手続き
- ☐ temporary injunction 仮差し止め命令、仮処分
- ☐ request ... to *do* …に〜するように要請する
- ☐ operator 運営者
- ☐ disclose 明らかにする、開示する
- ☐ IP address IPアドレス
- ☐ internet service provider インターネット接続事業者

7
- ☐ personal information 個人情報
- ☐ only after ... …したあとにようやく→このonlyは「ようやく、初めて」の意
- ☐ offender 違反者

8
- ☐ successfully うまく、首尾よく
- ☐ remain …のままである
- ☐ even if ... たとえ…だとしても
- ☐ manage to *do* 何とかして〜する
- ☐ obtain 入手する
- ☐ poster 投稿者
- ☐ prove 証明する
- ☐ right 権利
- ☐ infringe upon ... …を侵害する
- ☐ spread 拡散
- ☐ in order to *do* 〜するために
- ☐ device 機器
- ☐ internet cafe インターネットカフェ

Track 58

9 The cost of lawsuits poses another obstacle and the benefit of filing a lawsuit is limited since the average compensation in damages reportedly ranges from ¥300,000 to ¥600,000.

10 To simplify the procedure to identify offenders, an Internal Affairs and Communications Ministry panel on June 4 agreed that victims of cyberbullying should have the right to ask website and social media operators and internet service providers to disclose the names and phone numbers of people who make defamatory posts. Once phone numbers are obtained, lawyers can contact mobile operators and learn the identities of the individuals making the abusive posts. The government aims to revise the related laws as early as the end of the year.

Track 59

11 Another way to crack down on the problem would be to impose stricter regulations on online posts. Many experts, however, urge caution as doing so could restrict freedom of expression, and say that social media operators and website operators can play a greater role instead of the government.

12 Individual messages may not constitute illegality, but if tens of thousands of hate messages are made online against an individual, they can become a powerful weapon to psychologically ruin that person. Social media operators and website operators should create a system to prevent cyberbullying, such as giving people warnings or removing hate messages on their platforms.

9
- [ ] pose もたらす
- [ ] obstacle 妨げ
- [ ] benefit 利点
- [ ] compensation in damages 損害賠償額
- [ ] reportedly 伝えられるところでは
- [ ] range from A to B AからBにまで及ぶ、AからBまでの幅がある

10
- [ ] simplify 簡素化する
- [ ] Internal Affairs and Communications Ministry 総務省
- [ ] panel 委員会
- [ ] have the right to *do* ～する権利がある
- [ ] once いったん…すれば
- [ ] contact 連絡する
- [ ] mobile operator 携帯電話事業者
- [ ] identity 身元
- [ ] abusive 口汚い
- [ ] aim to *do* ～することを目指す
- [ ] revise 改正する
- [ ] related 関連のある

11
- [ ] crack down on ... …を厳しく取り締まる
- [ ] impose A on B AをBに課す
- [ ] strict 厳格な
- [ ] regulation 規制
- [ ] urge caution 警鐘を鳴らす
- [ ] restrict 制限する
- [ ] freedom of expression 表現の自由
- [ ] play a role 役割を果たす
- [ ] instead of ... …の代わりに

12
- [ ] individual 個々の→このindividualは形容詞
- [ ] constitute 構成する
- [ ] illegality 違法性、不法行為
- [ ] tens of thousands of ... 何万もの…
- [ ] weapon 武器
- [ ] psychologically 精神的に
- [ ] ruin 駄目にする、ずたずたにする
- [ ] warning 警告
- [ ] remove 取り除く
- [ ] platform プラットフォーム→基盤となるシステムのこと

13   Moreover, people should also learn how to use social media responsibly. In the United States, Trisha Prabhu a high school student, has invented an online app called "ReThink" that gives a pop-up alert if a message that the app user is writing contains offensive words. It gives them a chance to reconsider sending such words in an email, text or social media post. According to Ms. Prabhu's research, more than 93 percent of adolescents changed their minds and decided not to post the offensive message after reading the alert.

14   Ms. Prabhu described cyberbullying as "a silent pandemic affecting millions and millions of kids around the world." We must use our collective wisdom to overcome this scourge.

13
- □ moreover さらには
- □ responsibly 責任を持って
- □ invent 考案する
- □ app アプリ→applicationの略
- □ pop-up ポップアップの→ポップアップとは、コンピューター画面に別ウインドウとして(突然)現れる機能のこと

- □ alert 警告、アラート
- □ contain 含む
- □ offensive 侮辱的な
- □ reconsider 考え直す
- □ text テキストメッセージ
- □ according to ... …によると
- □ adolescent 若者

14
- □ describe 表現する
- □ millions and millions of ... 非常に多くの…→millions of ...(何百万もの…)を強調する表現

- □ collective 結集した
- □ wisdom 知恵
- □ overcome 克服する
- □ scourge 災厄

人口統計学的な難局との闘いを広げよ

1　年ごとの新生児の数が、若者たちが国の将来について抱く（家族を持てるだけの安心を感じるような）期待の指標だとしたら、日本の見通しはかなり厳しい。2019年にこの国で生まれた赤ん坊の推計数は、前の年から5万人以上減少して86万4,000人となり、過去120年間で最低であった。これは1970年代半ば、国の合計特殊出生率（一人の女性が生涯で出産する子どもの平均人数）が人口を維持するために必要な数値を最後に記録したときのおよそ40%に当たる。

2　高齢者が人口のより大きな割合を占めているため、昨年の死者数は戦後の最高記録となる137万人に達したと推計される。人口の自然減（死亡数から出生数を引いた数）は、51万2,000人とこれまた最高記録になった。日本はたった1年間で鳥取県（55万人）の人口に相当する人口を失ったのだ。悪い知らせは、国の人口の高齢化と縮小が今後数十年間で加速すると予測されていることである。

3　出生数が低下傾向にある日本の人口の急激な高齢化と減少の問題は、今に始まったことではない。1990年代以降、政府は保育サービスの定員を増大させるなど、若い夫婦の子育てを支援するための対策に取り組んできた。10月には3歳から5歳までの子どもたちに対して、無償の保育や幼児教育の提供を始めた。しかし、こうした努力は、減少する出生数という長期的な傾向を反転させる目に見える効果を生むことができなかった。それどころか、データはわが国の人口が以前に予測されていたよりも急激に高齢化と縮小が進行していることを示している。

4　政府の努力は依然として不十分である。日本は保育サービスや児童手当といった家族関連の公費にGDPの1.3%を費やしているが、これはより高い出生率を維持しているヨーロッパ諸国の水準のおよそ3分の1に当たる。しかし、過去数十年間の経験はまた、政府の政策だけでは流れを反転できないことを示唆している。

5　人口統計学的な難局に対処するためには、政府の政策の問題点を精査するとともに、子育てや家事の負担が女性に集中しがちな社会の仕組みの見直しから、父親と母親のどちらもが家族と一緒に過ごすことを妨げる慢性的な長時間労働などの、日本の会社に広く行き渡っている労働慣行の修正に至るまで、より広範囲に及ぶ取り組みが必要とされる。

6　子どもを持つという選択は各個人に委ねられるが、若者たちが金銭的な不安によって子どもを持つことを思いとどまらせられることのないような社会的・経済的環境を、少なくとも確保することが必要である。1990年代初めのバブル景気崩壊後に学校を卒業した「就職氷河期」世代の多くには、そのことが当てはまると考えられている。

7　減り続ける子どもの人口（これは結果として、来るべき数十年間における労働者要員の縮小につながるものとなるが）は、富を生成する能力を損ない、個人消費のベースを制限することにより、国の経済の将来的な成長を危険にさらす。生産年齢人口の減少（1995年の8716万人から2018年には7545万人に減り、2030年には6875万人、2040年には5978万人に減少すると予測されている）は、現役世代によって支払われる保険料が増加する高齢者層への給付金を賄う仕組みになっている社会保障制度の根幹を揺るがす。

8　高齢化と減少が進む人口は、これまでこの国を支えてきたさまざまな制度の持続をより困難にさせる。事態を複雑にしている要因は、国の47都道府県中で最も出生率が低い東京への人口流出である。「地方創生」のスローガンの下で傾向を反転させるとの政府の公約にもかかわらず、首都圏への正味の人口流入には依然として衰えが見られない。それほど遠くない将来には、多くの市区町村の存続そのものが疑わしくなることであろう。これらの地域では、現行の地方自治体の枠組みの下で住民に対する行政サービスを維持することが今後難しくなり、またその一方、地方の過疎化が進んだ地域にある多くの小さな市区町村は、地方自治の基盤そのものである議会の維持がますます困難になるという事態に直面している。

9　国の現在の人口統計学的な難局は1970年代からの長期的な傾向の結果で、人口のより一層の高齢化と縮小は避けられないと思われる（それは、出産適齢期の主要な層に属する女性の数がすでに著しく減少しているからだ）。2000年には25歳から39歳までの女性は1300万人いた。今日ではその数は970万人になっている。合計特殊出生率は史上最低に近い水準にとどまっていて、数値のささやかな回復では今後の数十年間で新生児数の減少と減り続ける人口を反転させることは期待できない。

人口統計学的な難局との闘いを広げよ

10 日本の人口の急激な高齢化と縮小への即効薬は存在しないが、何もしないことは状況をさらに悪化させるだけであろう。われわれは効果的な対策を模索・特定し、それらを着実に実行する必要がある。それと等しく重要なのは、国のさまざまな制度や政策を、手遅れになる前に人口統計学的な現実に合うよう手直しすることであろう。人口の高齢化に伴い、年金、医療サービス、高齢者介護といった年間の社会保障費は、2025年には140兆円に達し、人口の高齢化がピークに近づくと予測される2040年には190兆円にまで膨れ上がると見られている。必要な改革と手直しをこれらの制度に導入することは、国の将来に対する若い世代の不安感を和らげることに貢献するであろう。 （訳・注　桑田）

相模原障害者施設殺傷事件の背後にある問題

1 2016年7月、神奈川県相模原市の知的障害者のための介護福祉施設で19人を殺害し、ほかの多数の負傷者を出した罪に問われている植松聖被告に対して現在行われている裁判は、人がどれだけ社会にとって役に立つか、あるいは生産的であるかという基準に基づいて他人の人生の価値を判断しているのは果たして彼だけだろうか、とわれわれ全員があらためて考える機会を与えてくれるはずだ。

2 ほんの四半世紀前まで、わが国には「優生学的に劣った」子孫の誕生を防止することを目的に精神的障害を持った人々の強制不妊手術を認める法律が存在し、その法律の被害者に対する補償制度が法制化され、被害者たちに対し政府が謝罪したのはようやく昨年になってからのことだった。障害を持つ人々に対する差別はわが国の社会にいまだに根深く存在している。われわれは被害者に対する植松被告のゆがんだ、そして卑劣な考え方にのみ焦点を当てるのではなく、今回のおぞましい殺害事件の背後にある被告の考え方をいくらかでも社会全般が共有していないかどうかを真剣に考える必要がある。

3 4年前に介護施設の入所者に対し刃物による殺害事件を起こしたとして警察に出頭して以来ずっと、同施設の元職員である植松被告は自分は社会のためによかれと思って被害者たちを殺したが、それは重度の障害を持った人間は役立たずで、不幸しかもたらさないからであり、だから安楽死させるべきなのだ、と主張している。彼は先月始まった裁判でも同様の持論を繰り返してきた。彼は自分は裁判を受けるに足りる精神的に正常な責任能力を持っていると主張し、彼自身の弁護側から出された精神異常を根拠とした無罪の申し立てを退けている。

4 彼の言葉を自らの犯罪を正当化するための大量殺人犯のゆがんだ考え方だとして片付けてしまうのは簡単だろう。ただ、報道によると、殺害が行われて以来オンライン上に書き込まれた多数のメッセージは彼の考え方を支持しているらしい。これは障害を持った人々に対する偏見と差別が一般の人々の間でいまだに根強く残っていることの表れである。判決が3月半ばに言い渡される予定の横浜地裁での裁判員裁判は、植松被告がどのようにして彼のゆがんだものの考え方を抱くに至ったのかを詳しく探る必要がある。そして、われわれは社会全体がそのような考え方を退けるために何ができるかをじっくり考えなければならない。

5 知的障害や精神疾患、あるいは遺伝性疾患を持った人々の不妊化手術を、たとえ手術を受ける本人たちの同意がなくとも行うことを認める「優生保護法」が廃止さ

れたのは、ようやく1996年になってからのことだった。1948年に同法が制定されて以降、半世紀近くにわたって、合計およそ2万5,000人に対して手術が行われ、そのうち少なくとも1万6,500人に対しては本人の意思に反しての手術だったという。ところが、政府の政策によって子どもを持つ権利を奪われた被害者に対して国が救済措置と謝罪を与えるまでには、それから20年以上の歳月がかかったのである。

6 今日でさえ、生産的で社会にとって役立つかどうかという基準で、人とその価値を判断するものの考え方が残っている。優生保護法の被害者たち、そして医学的根拠もなく何十年も強制隔離を強いられた元ハンセン病患者たちを支援する人々は、被害者たちは、その存在が社会にとって都合の悪い人々を排除しようとする政府の誤った政策の犠牲者なのだと述べている。支援者たちが非難するところによると、相模原の介護施設で起こった殺害事件の背後にあるのは、日本政府がその政策を通じて広め、関連する法律が廃止された後でさえも根絶できなかった優生学的な信条なのだという。

7 2016年に今回の殺害事件が起こる直前に、行政機関や民間企業が障害を持った人々を差別することを禁じる法律が制定されていた。ところが内閣府が翌年行った調査によると、回答者の80%以上がそのような差別や偏見が社会に根強く残っていると思うと答えている。知的障害や精神障害を持った人々のための介護施設を建設する計画はしばしば近隣住民からの反対に直面し、その結果、そうした計画の中には最終的に中止に追い込まれるものも出ている。2016年に相模原市の介護施設で起きた殺害事件の犠牲者の大部分が、裁判では氏名が非公開になっている事実もまた、あまりにも多くの人々が障害者やその家族に対して抱いているゆがんだ見方をわれわれに思い出させるものである。

8 障害を持った人々に対する忌まわしい犯罪の再発を防止する一助とするためには、社会全体がそのような人々に対して広く持たれている偏見や差別に正面から取り組み、その状況を改善する方策を取る必要がある。　　　　　（訳・注　小川）

見直すべき核燃料サイクルの探求

1 先月、西日本の原子炉2基から（軽水炉でのプルトニウム・ウラン燃料の商業的利用が約10年前に開始されて以来初めて）取り出された使用済み混合酸化物（MOX）燃料の不確かな運命は、政府の核燃料サイクル政策をめぐる行き詰まりをまたしても示すものである。政府は使用済み核燃料がすべて原子炉の燃料として再利用するために再処理されると主張するが、この国には使用済みMOX燃料を再処理できる施設がないため、原子力発電所の貯蔵プールに無期限にとどまることになる。

2 青森県六ヶ所村に建設中の日本原燃株式会社が所有する再処理工場は、使用済みウラン燃料しか扱えない。使用済みMOX燃料の再処理能力がある2つ目の工場を建設するための具体的な計画はこれまで一切立てられていない。六ヶ所村の工場自体の完成も、1990年代初めに建設が始まって以来、膨大なコストの超過をもたらした技術的な不具合が絶えず連続する中にあって、何年も遅れている。工場が完成し、操業を開始しても、おそらく日本のプルトニウム備蓄量を増やすだけになるであろう。これは東京電力ホールディングス株式会社が運営していた福島第一原子力発電所での2011年の炉心融解後、運転を停止した原子炉の再稼働が遅いため、MOX燃料におけるプルトニウムの使用が低調なままとどまっているからである。

3 核燃料サイクル政策についての難しい決断をこれ以上先送りする代わりに、政府と電力業界は政策の見通しを公正に評価し、延び延びになっている見直しを進める必要がある。

4 ウラン資源の有効利用をうたう政策の下、原子力発電所で使い終わった燃料集合体は、プルトニウムを抽出するために原子炉から取り出され、そのプルトニウムがMOX燃料を作るためにウランと混合される。1月に愛媛県にある四国電力株式会社伊方発電所および福井県にある関西電力株式会社高浜発電所の原子炉から取り出されたのは、2010年に装荷されたMOX燃料棒である。使用済みMOX燃料を再処理することは科学技術的に実現可能であると政府は主張するが、専門家はこの方式の効率に関して疑問を抱いている。

5 当初、政策は日本の原子力発電における高速増殖炉への移行を想定していた。燃料として消費するよりも多くのプルトニウムを生成するとうたわれた高速増殖炉は、資源の乏しいこの国において夢の技術であると思われた。しかし、国の唯一の高速増殖原型炉で、1兆円以上が費やされた「もんじゅ」は、一連の事故やトラ

見直すべき核燃料サイクルの探求

ブルのため、1994年に初めて稼働して以降のほとんどの期間、運転を停止していた後、2016年に廃炉になった。政府はフランスとの共同プロジェクトで次世代高速炉の研究を継続しようと努めたが、ウラン資源の豊富さがその経済的可能性に疑問を投げ掛けたことを考慮して、フランス政府がプロジェクトを大幅に縮小することを決定して以来、取り組みは中ぶらりんの状態にある。

6　六ヶ所村の再処理工場の完成が先延ばしにされ続けているので、1万5,000トンほどの使用済み核燃料が日本各地の原子力発電所で保管されている。六ヶ所村の工場の貯蔵プールにある3,000トンと合わせると、総量はおよそ1万8,000トンに達する。再処理工場の操業開始がない中でより多くの原子炉が再稼働されれば、その量は増える一方であろうし、原発の貯蔵プールの容量は限られている。

7　その一方で、拡散への懸念のため、日本は45トンのプルトニウムの備蓄を燃料として活用する必要に迫られている。もんじゅのプロジェクトが行き詰まったため、政府と電力業界は2010年ごろから、従来型の軽水炉でのMOX燃料の使用を追求してきた。けれども、2011年の福島での大惨事後、国の原発の大半の運転停止を受けて、MOX燃料の使用は遅々として進んでいない。現在、MOX燃料は全国でわずか4基の原子炉でしか使用されておらず、それは福島での事故以前に計画されていた16基から18基をはるかに下回っている。従来の核燃料よりも費用がかかるMOX燃料の使用の経済的可能性についての疑問もある。

8　核燃料サイクル政策が行き詰まっているのは明らかなように思えるが、政府も電力業界もそのことを認めないだろう。それは、計画の放棄は原子力エネルギー政策に深刻な影響を及ぼすと見られるからだ。再処理の代案は使用済み燃料を地中深くに埋めることで、伝えられるところでは、この方法はいくつかの国で採用されている。とはいえ、そうなると、これまで再利用のために処理される資源として保管されてきた使用済み燃料は核廃棄物と化すことになり、それをどこに処分するかという政治的に慎重な対応を要する問題が発生する。だが、日本の原子力利用を考えると、それは避けられない問題だ。実現し難い核燃料サイクルの探求を続けるための口実として、そのことを使用するべきではない。今こそ政策を見直すべき時である。

（訳・注　桑田）

ネット上の中傷は多くを苦しめる静かなパンデミック

1 人気のリアリティー番組『テラスハウス』に出演していた22歳のプロレスラーの木村花さんが、何百もの嫌がらせのメッセージを受け取ったあとに自殺したとされるニュースは、先月下旬、日本中に衝撃を与えた。政府がネットいじめの被害者保護に向けた対策を取るのが遅れていることを思い起こさせる、悲劇的な出来事であった。

2 「こうしたコメントをネット上で読まなければいいだけだと言う人もいます。けれども、ソーシャルメディアは私たちの生活の欠かせない一部になっていて、それらを見ないでいることは極めて難しいのです」。ジャーナリストで、日本の「#MeToo」運動の象徴的存在である伊藤詩織氏は、最近の記者会見でそう述べた。

3 TBSテレビの山口敬之・元ワシントン支局長に対する性被害の告発を公表してから、伊藤氏は3年以上にわたってネット上で嫌がらせのメッセージを受け続けている。嫌がらせのメッセージの中には、彼女の家族や友人に向けられたものもあった。ネット上のおよそ70万件のメッセージを丹念に調べた後、伊藤氏は月曜日、ツイッター上で名誉を傷付けたとして、漫画家のはすみとしこ氏とほかの2人に対する訴えを起こした。伊藤氏は、はすみ氏の漫画は伊藤氏が虚偽の性被害を告発し、その被害者を装っていると示唆して名誉を傷付けたと主張している。

4 今日、ますます多くの人がソーシャルメディアを利用するにつれ、ネットいじめは命に関わる恐れのある懸念事項として浮上している。政府とソーシャル・ネットワーキング・サービス(SNS)がネット上の中傷を防ぐための効果的な対策を打ち出すべき時である。

5 そうした中傷がはびこる主な理由の一つは、中傷的な投稿を匿名でネットに上げられることで、しかも複雑な手順が関係してくるため、投稿者を見つけることはほとんど不可能である。

6 日本でそのような個人の身元を特定するためには、被害者は複数の訴訟手続きを経なければならない。まず、被害者は裁判所に対して、中傷的なメッセージを投稿した個人のIPアドレスを開示するよう、ツイッターなどのSNS事業者に要請する仮処分を求めなければならない。IPアドレスを特定することで、メッセージを投稿するためにどのインターネット接続事業者が使用されたのかを、被害者は突き止めることができる。

ネット上の中傷は多くを苦しめる静かなパンデミック

7 次に被害者は、そのインターネット接続事業者に名前や住所などの個人情報を開示するよう要請するための訴訟を起こさなければならない。この手続きを経てようやく、被害者は加害者に対して訴訟を起こすことができる。

8 それぞれの段階をうまく踏んでいくことも、依然として難しいままである。たとえば、被害者が投稿者のIPアドレスを何とか入手できたとしても、インターネット接続事業者から個人情報を入手するためには、投稿の拡散によって自身の権利が侵害されたことを証明しなければならない。投稿がインターネットカフェのパソコンなど、複数の人間によって使用されている機器から上げられたものならば、誰が投稿したのかを特定することはほぼ不可能である。

9 訴訟費用がもう一つの妨げになっていて、平均の損害賠償額も伝えられるところでは30万円から60万円かかるため、訴訟を起こすことの利点も限定されている。

10 加害者を特定する手続きを簡素化するために、総務省の委員会は6月4日、ネットいじめの被害者にはウェブサイトやソーシャルメディアの運営者、およびインターネット接続事業者に対して、中傷的な投稿をネットに上げている人物の名前と電話番号を開示するように求める権利があるべきだということで意見が一致した。電話番号が得られれば、弁護士は携帯電話事業者に連絡して、口汚い投稿をする個人の身元を教えてもらうことができる。政府は早ければ年末に、関連する法律を改正することを目指している。

11 この問題を厳しく取り締まるもう一つの方法は、ネット上の投稿に対してより厳格な規制を課すことであろう。けれども、多くの専門家はそうすることで表現の自由を制限しかねないと警鐘を鳴らしていて、政府ではなくソーシャルメディア運営者やウェブサイト運営者がより大きな役割を果たすことができると述べている。

12 一つ一つのメッセージは違法に当たらないかもしれないが、何万もの悪意あるメッセージがネット上で個人に対して発せられると、その人を精神的に破滅させる強力な武器になりかねない。ソーシャルメディア運営者とウェブサイト運営者は、利用者に警告を与える、もしくは嫌がらせのメッセージを自身のプラットフォームから削除するといった、ネットいじめを防ぐためのシステムを構築するべきである。

13　さらには、利用者も責任を持ってソーシャルメディアを使う方法を学ぶべきである。米国では、高校生のトリーシャ・プラブさんが、「ReThink」と呼ばれるオンラインアプリを開発した。これはアプリのユーザーの書いているメッセージが侮辱的な言葉を含んでいると、ポップアップの警告を表示するものである。Eメールやテキストメッセージ、またはソーシャルメディアの投稿でそうした単語を送信することを、ユーザーに考え直す機会を与えてくれる。プラブさんの調査によると、93％以上の若者たちが警告を読んだあとに考えを変え、侮辱的なメッセージを投稿しないことにしたという。

14　プラブさんはネットいじめを「世界中の非常に多くの子どもたちを苦しめる静かなパンデミック」と表現する。われわれはこの災厄を克服するために英知を結集しなければならない。　　　　　　　　　　　　　　　　　　　　（訳・注　桑田）

ジャパンタイムズ社説集
—2020年上半期

2020年9月5日　初版発行

編　者　ジャパンタイムズ出版 英語出版編集部
　　　　© The Japan Times Publishing, Ltd., 2020
監　修　又江原 裕
発行者　伊藤 秀樹
発行所　株式会社 ジャパンタイムズ出版
　　　　〒102-0082 東京都千代田区一番町 2-2 一番町第二 TGビル2F
　　　　電話　050-3646-9500（出版営業部）
　　　　ウェブサイト　https://jtpublishing.co.jp/
印刷所　日経印刷株式会社

本書の内容に関するお問い合わせは、上記ウェブサイトまたは郵便でお受けいたします。

定価はカバーに表示してあります。

万一、乱丁落丁のある場合は送料当社負担でお取り替えいたします。
（株）ジャパンタイムズ出版・出版営業部宛てにお送りください。

ISBN978-4-7890-1770-1
Printed in Japan

読者アンケートのご案内
〜ご感想・ご意見をお待ちしております〜

ジャパンタイムズ出版のコーポレートサイトが新しくなりました。
本書のご感想・ご意見をぜひお寄せください。

アンケートURL

https://jtpublishing.co.jp/contact/comment/

本ページで読者の声を紹介いたします。
掲載された方には **QUOカードPay 500円分**を
プレゼント！

Present!